Timeless Advice
for Parents of
Young Children

Timeless Advice for Parents of Young Children

from the Grandmothers of Hanna Perkins Center

How to Understand Your Child's Behavior and
Respond Effectively in Almost Any Situation

Kathy Baker, Maria Kaiser,
Georgianna Roberts, Ginny Steininger
and consultant Barbara Streeter

Illustrations by Maria Kaiser

Hanna Perkins Center for Child Development
Shaker Heights, Ohio

Hanna Perkins Center for Child Development
hannaperkins.org

ISBN 978-0-692-16000-8

Printed in the United States of America

To Lainie Hadden,
who believed in us enough
to make us think we
could write a book.

Contents

PART THREE

FEELINGS SPEAK LOUDER THAN WORDS

PART FOUR

SELF ESTEEM CANNOT BE PURCHASED

PART FIVE

THEY CRAWL BEFORE THEY WALK

Introduction

We talk about the good old days when mothers could with impunity shout at their children, "You're driving me crazy; go outside and play!" These days a mom is more likely to say, "Now in five minutes I'm going to have to ask you to turn off your iPad because it's almost time for soccer practice." Where did this generation of superparents come from? After all, they're *our* children, who learned parenting from us, the same way we learned parenting from our parents. Only while we in our ignorance—and innocence—just let history repeat itself, our kids are raising their kids very differently from the way they were brought up. What happened here? And is it all bad?

Well, of course not. We're grateful, for example, that our grandchildren have mothers with educations and careers and jobs—including child rearing—that are considered just as important as their fathers.' We're glad that their families are seen as democracies, not dictatorships ruled by a patriarch or matriarch, and where household tasks are shared by both parents. We appreciate the way our children acknowledge and listen to their children's opinions, although we have to admit that we still think "Because I'm the parent and you're the kid" is sometimes a perfectly good answer to "Why?"

Times have changed, all right, but if one thing is certain, it's that there's no going back, as much as we'd like to. Mothers might want to send their kids out to play in the neighborhood the way they did as children, but if they did, whom would their kids play with? Fathers might resent having to spend hours and hours helping their kids with their school projects, but if they don't, they'll feel guilty because all the other fathers are helping *their* kids. Maybe a creative thinker would be able to figure out an alternative, but most of us don't have the time or energy to challenge the status quo.

However, some things never change. There are actually a few basic unchanging truths about what young children need beyond food and shelter. That's what this book is all about: the things that don't change because what's best for kids has not changed, will never change. *And how do we old ladies know what those things are?* you might ask.

Well, first of all, we are older than you are. We've lived longer, had more experiences, learned more. For what that's worth. (When you're over 75, which we all are, you think that's worth a lot.) But we are not ordinary grandmothers who have raised only our own children and grandchildren. As early childhood professionals, we have helped other people raise their children, in preschools and child care centers, for many years as teachers in and directors of a variety of early childhood programs. In addition, we all have degrees in early childhood education. And maybe what's most important, we've gained insights into young children's behavior by studying together with Erna Furman, a noted child analyst and child development expert at the Hanna Perkins Center for Child Development. She taught us not only about how children feel, but about how parents feel, with what we experienced as divine authority.

It took us four lifetimes to write these simple pieces. We didn't start writing them until we were in our 60s. Then we began sending articles to parenting magazines, writing answer columns for a community newspaper, creating pamphlets for distribution in child care centers and pediatricians' offices, writing a blog for the Cleveland *Plain Dealer*. We discussed each piece among ourselves and with our adviser, Barbara Streeter, but we wrote them individually, so you will recognize four different writing styles and points of view. But throughout we hope you'll sense a consistent awareness of how difficult parenting can be. Especially in this age of breathtakingly accelerated change.

We really do know what is best for young children. Please note: *young* children. Don't bring us your adolescents with their very different issues and problems (although we say with conviction that if you take our advice in the early years, you will have a better chance of surviving the teen ones).

Another caveat: We write about emotional growth, not physical or intellectual. It's up to you to get your kid into Harvard or standing on an Olympic podium with a gold medal around his neck.

But actually, that's one of the things we want to talk to you about: You young parents seem to believe that it's your responsibility to get your children into the very best schools while winning the most desirable prizes. We hate to see you assuming that each toileting accident and scribbled picture predicts a dark future where your children fail even to get into a college that nobody ever heard of, or to secure minimally gainful employment. You seem to think that you are in control of these small lives that have been placed in your hands and that you are a failure as a parent if you don't make existence for them one long string of successes. Or, at the very least, days of endless joy and entertainment. Your impulses are not all wrong, not at all. You are like good parents have always been: You want to protect your children from all harm. And in so doing you want to protect yourself from the pain of seeing your children cry, watching your children fail. We are here to tell you that quite possibly you aren't in control at all, but that there are a number of practical things you can learn that will make raising your children less of an anxious struggle.

They are based on some unchanging truths. Truth number one, of course: Being a Parent is Hard. Raising kids has never been and will never be unmitigated joy. Read in Part One about those times when being a parent is hard: Your child is afraid; your child is sad; your child shocks you by hurting other children; your child drives you nuts with whining and complaining.

Truth number two: Being a Child is Hard. They've never been here before, so we can't expect them to think the way we do, nor perceive reality in the same way. Part Two helps us see into the ways their small brains work—what they are capable of understanding and what they are not.

Truth number three: Self Esteem Cannot Be Purchased. Not with litanies of praise ("Good job!") or actual medals and trophies. Self-esteem comes from accomplishments that children master on their own.

Number four: Feelings Speak Louder than Words. Those are your feelings we're talking about. Your child is quick to sense how you are feeling, and if you are saying one thing but feeling another, your child will know it. If you acknowledge your own feelings, you'll be better able to recognize your child's.

Number five: They Crawl Before They Walk. There are exceptions, but the ages and stages of child development haven't changed through the years and are predictable. Don't expect toddler behavior of an infant, and don't think your toddler should "know better" than to bite a playmate.

Number six: Only Once a Child. There are no do-overs for childhood, so don't be rushing your kids through theirs. This is also a catch-all category for everything that's left over. All that we know about what's best for kids can't always be neatly categorized.

There is one final truth: that everyone's going to survive this. Our children survived what now is viewed as negligence if not outright neglect, and their children will survive what our generation sometimes sees as overindulgence and gross permissiveness. The world may be going to hell in a handbasket, but it hasn't gotten there yet. We Grandmothers are willing to risk saying that it never will as long as there are loving parents and grandparents, skilled child-development professionals, and a fresh new generation of babies for whom "The Eency Weency Spider" is a brand-new song.

PART ONE

Being a Parent Is Hard

Being a Parent Has Always Been Hard

Maybe this is the main gift that we Grandmothers can give the current generation of parents, the acknowledgment that parenting can be messy, wearying, frustrating. You aren't a bad parent if you would like to throw your screaming baby out the window, we tell them. You're only a bad parent if you actually do it. And you can admit to that urge; it's perfectly OK. Parents have always felt and always will have those feelings of aggression, along with alternating and sometimes layered feelings of helplessness, exhaustion, guilt, and above all, a love so intense that sometimes it hurts.

Being a parent is hard, but you are making it harder than it needs to be if you are turning it into a competitive sport. You don't have to be the best parent on the block; there's no such thing. People have been parents since Cain and Abel were born, but "parenting," as a verb and a job title, didn't even exist when we Grandmothers were so employed. The pressure to be perfect parents was unknown to us when our children were small, and we wish we could will you to ignore it.

Your instincts are good; follow them. With our empathy and a modicum of advice.

Picky Eaters

Kids today are probably not any pickier about eating than those of previous generations. Don't you remember slipping your mystery meat under the table to the dog, or hiding Brussels sprouts in your napkin so you could flush them down the toilet?

But it does seem that children today are more outspoken about what they don't like, and that their parents feel compelled to serve as short-order cooks for them. We have to assume that many parents are not happy with this situation, however, and would prefer it if their children showed a willingness to try new flavors, rather than watching mealtime become an exchange of whines and threats over the food that has been served.

Eating is one of the few areas in which children can exert their autonomy—you can put it in front of them, but you can't make them eat it!—and so they may insist on their right to refuse anything that looks or smells strange to them. And with their smaller bodies and appetites, some children may just not be very hungry, especially when they've reached a plateau between growth spurts, and most especially when someone serves them a mountainous portion and insists they eat it. All of it. Because it's good for them.

Forgive me if I insert a sidebar here. We Grannies think you offer your children way too many between-meal snacks. We are amazed to see you filling a backpack with juice boxes and crackers just for a trip to the post office. Maybe that's why your child doesn't want to eat at mealtime—he's full of apple juice and Goldfish crackers.

Parents of picky eaters can get frustrated, even panicky, because there are few instincts more basic than feeding our young. We want to see our child nourished and healthy, and instead he sits there (look how skinny he is!) listlessly pushing the food around his plate. We alternate between wanting to force-feed him and offering to get him something else, any-thing else, so that he might actually consume a few calories.

But the more we beg, cajole or insist, the more determined the child becomes not to eat.

Make a new family rule: Absolutely no arguing about food. Food is not to be mentioned at mealtime, except to ask that something be passed or to compliment the cook or to say how delicious the asparagus is this time of year. Mealtime is to be pleasant, with conversation devoted to sharing ideas and obser-vations. Pretend not to notice what someone eats or doesn't eat. Don't acknowledge a child's new or longstanding aversion to a particular food (setting up a self-fulfilling prophecy), and don't praise him for overcoming it (he shouldn't learn to eat to please you). Never offer alternative menu choices except for an agreed-upon backup food—for example, a banana—that a child can get for himself.

Let the child serve his own plate, if he is able, so that the portion will be one of his choosing. At the end of the meal, if he has eaten little to nothing, so be it. Because you have made another family rule that is a corollary to the first: He can help himself to the healthy foods available in the vegetable drawer in the refrigerator or on the bottom shelf of the cupboard.

Parents might try to engage their children's interest and assistance in menu-planning, grocery shopping and cooking. And aim always for an actual family mealtime, when everyone sits down to eat at once to enjoy the conversation and togetherness. This may be difficult to arrange every day, but parents can make that their goal rather than somehow getting some food down the picky eater.

KSB

Tantrums

Parents of preschoolers often ask us about temper tantrums. It's a stage they'd like to get through as quickly as possible. Tantrums most often occur in public places like supermarkets and shopping malls. They are characterized by screaming and thrashing, and if the parent starts screaming and thrashing herself, matters only get worse.

Most tantrums are caused by helpless rage. The child wants what he wants with great intensity and in his smallness feels powerless in the face of some obstacle or an adult's "no." He cannot project into the future, can only see the now, and feels as if he is drowning in grief at having been denied what he wants. At the same time, he is murderously furious at the cause of his frustration. His own rage can terrify him because he is often lashing out at the person he most loves and depends on, and it can escalate into full-blown hysteria. In addition, a child who has been rewarded in the past by his parent's giving in to the tantrum—quickly supplying the candy or balloon or whatever the child was so loudly demanding—may begin to use tantrums manipulatively. He learns that tantrums can be uniquely effective, especially those conducted in a public setting.

Embarrassed and frustrated, you probably would like to pick your child up and shake him or walk away and leave him there kicking and frothing, or shove one of those lollipops he wants so desperately into his mouth—anything to make him stop screaming! But since you obviously would rather not do any of those things, you are tempted to resort to scary and empty threats, withdrawal of attention (which can feel like withdrawal of love), furtive arm-squeezing and lecturing through clenched teeth. Pull yourself together and don't do any of those, either.

The child has lost all reason, all control, and cannot possibly respond to reminders or reprimands. He is in a howling wilderness of emotions and can scarcely hear your voice.

So contain the child to the degree this is possible. Hold him, murmuring soothing sounds, assuring him that this will end and you are there to help. Carry him out of the shopping mall and sit awhile on the curb or in the car until the sobs begin to subside. Picture yourself as a warm blanket there to protect him from the storm until it passes. Only then do you begin to talk, to go over what happened, to try to remember together the incident that led to the tantrum. This sounds very time-consuming, but in the long run it will save you hours of repeat performances.

What to say afterward depends on the cause of the tantrum.

If sparked by rage: "You were feeling very angry with me for not buying you that candy, weren't you? You were so angry that you started crying and you couldn't stop. That must have been very scary. I bet you hope that doesn't happen again."

If manipulative: "I think when you screamed and cried in the store because I wouldn't buy candy for you, you thought that your crying would make me change my mind. It didn't work, did it? It isn't going to work next time, either. Let's talk about more big-boy ways for you to tell me what you want."

If possible, avoid tantrum-producing circumstances in the first place. But if you have to return to the scene of the tantrum, prepare your child in advance. Tell him that he can help you select some plums or apples for a snack, and that the candy in the check-out line is still going to be there, but that you aren't going to buy any this time. Then keep your word! With an older child, you might appeal to his desire to be more grown-up and avoid the embarrassment of public tantrums.

Some morning you will wake up and realize that your child hasn't thrown a tantrum in a long time. Hard to believe, but we Grandmothers can almost guarantee it.

KSB

Power Struggles

The room was strewn with Lego blocks and pieces from a game 4-year-old Aaron had been playing with. His mom sighed and wondered, "What will I try this time?" She squelched her urge to yell and threaten again; this had gotten her nowhere, just left her with a headache and sore throat. Bribery and cajoling worked occasionally, but those methods didn't feel right. They seemed to give Aaron too much power. His father, at the end of his rope, had spanked him and he had eventually picked up his toys, but everyone felt wiped out. Mom had even considered ignoring the mess, letting the toys accumulate or become broken. That would teach him! But would it really?

What was this all about anyway? Aaron had been defiant in other ways lately. Often, he refused to come when called and dawdled when it was time to go to bed or get dressed for pre-school. Sometimes he openly disobeyed his mother and father, but, often could be loving, helpful and fun to be with. Other times when his mother and father requested something of him, he could be very stubborn.

Most young children exhibit these behaviors as they strive to become independent individuals. As children acquire mobility and speech, they are also compelled to assert themselves in ways that can result in clashes of wills. If these clashes are part of the growing-up process, how can they be handled so that they become learning situations rather than angry standoffs?

Children must learn about dangers and how to avoid them. They need to learn to be responsible for their own actions. They must learn that others have feelings, rights and needs. In the heat of the child's disobedience, the parent's impulse to control the child takes over. But for children to learn self-control from their experiences, they need to be shown how their behaviors will adversely affect what they want for themselves.

"Pick them up now!" is overwhelming to a child surveying a room strewn with toys. The task seems impossible. He is unable to think beyond the interruption of his play, and unable to consider, on his own, what might happen if the toys are left out. Rather than establishing who's in charge, Mom or Dad can make the request seem manageable and reasonable. "Come on, I'll help you. There are a lot of toys on the floor and we don't want anyone to trip on them. I know how bad you'll feel if your toys get lost or broken or if somebody falls. That's why it's important to pick up your things—so that you can have fun with them again." This response helps the child learn and encourages a sense of responsibility. With Mom or Dad there beside him, the job won't seem so overwhelming.

It is usually not an act of defiance when a child doesn't come when called or ignores a request. A young child isn't yet equipped to consider the passage of time and others' schedules. She is in her own here-and-now. Warnings are more helpful: "In five more minutes, it will be time to clean up," or "Get dressed," "Turn off the TV," etc. Showing her where the big hand on the clock will be when five minutes are up will help her understand time and give her a tool that can help her feel in charge of herself, rather than feeling imposed upon.

Of course, there will always be occasions when the child will still dig in stubbornly and defy a request, even after reasonable explanations and supportive words. If after the five-minute warning and a couple of reasonable reminders there is still no move to turn off the TV, the parents could give the child a choice. "It looks as though you want me to be the boss of turning off the TV. You're really a big girl who could be her own boss of that. Shall I do it, or would you rather do it for yourself?"

There will be other instances when an older child may dig in his heels when asked to comply with a parent's request. Parents may have to resort to doing the task themselves while telling him that they will have to store away the toys he refuses to take care of for a while—or, there will be no TV for tomorrow if there is a fuss about turning it off—or, there will be no story at bedtime if he cannot be in his pjs when the clock says it's time. Don't forget to tell him how nice it is when he is able to do it of his own free will.

On a more positive note, eventually the child will learn that being in charge of his own behavior is better for everyone.

GS

Whining and Complaining

"**S**top that right now!"
   "If you don't stop that whining, I'll give you something real to whine about!"

   "If you complain about one more thing, you'll go to your room!"

   Listening to a child's persistent moaning and crying can make the most patient parents feel frenzied and helpless. They want it to stop—*now!*

   They want to exert their authority—make the child change and feel their power and control over him. After all, they are the adults! If they are in public, they feel embarrassed or inadequate and speak through clenched teeth: "Just wait 'til we get home!"

   It helps to understand what causes this behavior. Something as simple as being tired and staying up past his normal bedtime can make a child cranky and whiny. However, chronic whining and complaining usually comes from an accumulation of circumstances that leave the child dissatisfied and unable to comfort himself. We sometimes chalk up his whininess to "wanting attention," but it's usually more. A pestering child can be in the parent's presence with his physical needs being met yet still feel that his parent has left him. Whining is often an attempt to reclaim a parent's focus and support.

When whining is a reaction to the helpless "little" feeling that overtakes the child when he feels left out, he is letting you know how miserable he is. Even though the child's behavior at this point makes even the most laid-back parent frustrated and miserable, too, we can be sure that the child's frustration with himself is many times greater. He can't like himself when he behaves this way and is at a complete loss as to how to make things better. Ironically, just when you least feel like giving it, he needs his parents' love and support now more than ever. Helping a child overcome this miserable state will not be accomplished easily or quickly.

No matter what the cause of the present struggle, the first step is to re-establish connection with the child. The most immediate and effective method is a hug or a protective arm around her. Tell her you do get angry with her when she whines and complains, but you still love her. At the same time, tell her in a loving, happy way that you know she is unhappy and that you will help her figure out how both of you can feel better.

You also need to point out firmly that talking in a whiny voice will not get him what he thinks he wants. He needs to know that you'll stick to your word but that you will talk with him when he can use his "bigger-boy" voice. Give him a chance to take this in, but stop him if he goes back to the same old behavior. It's a hard job for him, so try to be patient. Saying "No!" firmly and not giving in will help stop what could become a nasty habit.

Later, if you can pinpoint some of the circumstances that

seem to bring on whininess, point them out to your child. "It seems you get cranky whenever I'm on the phone," or ". . . when it's time to stop something you're doing," or ". . . when you want something we say you cannot have," etc. Make a simple plan of what the child can do for herself when one of these times occurs—something that would help her feel close to you without interrupting or interfering, or that she could do until she can have your full attention or help.

Try to be observant of those times when your child *can* wait to do or have something he wants, and when he can overcome frustration without complaining. Express your appreciation for his figuring out things for himself. Let him know how that makes both of you feel better, and how nice it is to be able to have fun together instead of fighting. Note the times when your responsibilities and needs may make your child feel left out or disconnected from you. Show him that even though you may have to be doing other things or be in other places, you can know what he is doing and you're thinking of him.

GS

Sneakiness

Who among us can honestly claim to have never been sneaky if we define it as doing something forbidden, on the sly?

Sneakiness and lying in young children often infuriates parents and teachers. It's interesting that in adulthood our own sneaky histories are not only remembered in great detail but often humorously shared with friends. We remember exactly what we did and whether we were caught or got away with it. It was the guilt that imprinted these memories.

A while ago I visited a friend and her family. One afternoon I found myself in the kitchen with Janine, her lively little 4-year-old. She was playing with a puzzle, I was helping prepare dinner, and her mother had gone into the garden. She suddenly looked around and pushed a small stool against the cupboards. She glanced behind, climbed up and reached to the back of the shelf from which she pulled a chocolate. Holding it tightly, she jumped back to the floor, pushed the stool back to its proper position and hurried over to her play area. The chocolate was hastily unwrapped and devoured and the wrapper was immediately buried in the garbage can. She returned to her puzzle. I was a visitor and knew full well by the look on her face and her hurried and furtive movements that the hidden candy was out of bounds, and this little girl knew it. I neither said nor did anything.

In retrospect, I should have immediately wondered if she was into something she should not have been and that maybe Mommy had warned her not to eat the candy. I should have suggested that she'd feel bad if she did something she knew Mommy wouldn't like. Instead, I watched with fascination as she found an inventive, rather athletic way to reach the forbidden candy. The truth of the matter was that now we both felt guilty—Janine for breaking a rule even if she didn't get caught, and I, for allowing it to happen without some gentle, adult intervention.

It's unwise to accuse a 5-year-old of being a sneak or if, when caught and she denies it, a liar. These are strong words to use and aren't any help; nor is it helpful to look the other way, as did I. Adults rightly feel an obligation to discourage children from being sneaky or telling lies, and there are lessons to be taught about rules and the truth. Nothing is to be gained by severely punishing them when they transgress.

Severe admonitions simply result in a small child's trying to survive the fear of a parent's anger or the possibility of being spanked rather than feeling bad about what he or she had done and regretting it. Terrifying children with angry words and punishment might well drive them further into more inventive sneakiness, lying, and more creative ways to avoid being caught.

Young children's sneakiness can be attributed to wanting

something that is missing or forbidden, an urge they have that can't be satisfied. Their wishes are very strong at this young age, and having them denied results in angry feelings. They feel they haven't been able to get enough when being above-board with Mom and Dad so the impulse to get what they want trumps the newly learned rules and all other feelings.

When caught, young children often lie. It's an indication that they wish they had done the right thing or feel uncomfortable about what they have done. They really don't want to deliberately deceive others in order to "get away" with their forbidden acts. Believe it or not, lying can often be a confession because the discomfort of a sneaky act is almost more than they can bear.

By four years of age, Janine already knew many of the family rules, one of which was that candy was not to be taken without permission. She knew her mother would be angry and would certainly scold her had she been caught midtheft. She also predicted that if she had asked, she would have been denied the candy.

So how to approach your young child when you're sure this sneaky behavior will land her in prison one day? Contrary to the way I reacted to Janine's behavior by saying nothing, it would have been far more helpful for me to talk to her about taking something forbidden and about how bad she would feel inside if she did.

Recognizing with her how much she wanted the forbidden candy, for example, and how hard it was not to grab that piece when no one was looking might have helped her hear me. Suggesting we talk to Mom about a time when she might have a piece would be important. If she can't have any, it would be best to make that clear and find a substitute food or activity.

Approval by parents is very powerful for young children. So much depends on this strong relationship and a child's wish to keep it close. It often leads to children denying themselves something they badly want just to maintain it. At first it works when the parents are nearby but not when they are absent— it's for this reason babysitters can have difficulty with a child's behavior. Eventually it becomes the child's job to keep the rules in mind even in the absence of his parents.

So take heart and don't fret if your young preschooler takes a wrapped chocolate from the shelf when she thinks you're not watching, or if she denies it if caught. Try not to accuse her or jump to conclusions. Also be aware that nighttime fears often show up as a sign of your child's inner worries about naughtiness or temptations. Alone in bed, these forbidden acts surface, and she fears punishment. As hard as it is, allow her to let you know when she has been sneaky or has lied and do your best to keep the communication open.

With your help, as your child gets older, the rules will be remembered and her behavior will be modified. If all goes well, when she is five or six, her conscience will be all-powerful, and she will be consumed with rules and whether things are fair. It's a big developmental step for your child, and you can take pride in how she then begins to manage these temptations. Any need to be sneaky or to lie when caught will eventually diminish or disappear.

MLK

When Kids Don't Listen

Dear Grandmothers,

I find myself telling my kids the same things over and over again, but they don't seem to pay any attention. It would almost be better if they openly defied me. Instead, everything I say seems to be going in one ear and out the other. Why don't they listen to me?

—Unheard Mother

Dear Unheard,

As with so many of the issues we discuss with parents about those very complex little people, their children, the answers are many and varied. But from the top:

• Maybe your children are so bombarded by sounds—from the TV, radio, CD player, microwave, dishwasher, hair dryer, passing traffic, neighbor's leaf blower, etc.—that they have become very accomplished at shutting a lot of it out, including your voice. One thing you could do about that is not permit the TV, radio, or handheld gaming device to run constantly, to cut down on unnecessary background noise. That might help.

• Or maybe you don't always listen to them, either. What gets priority, them or the ringing cell phone?

• But probably it's not so simple. Do they seem to listen, then simply fail to finish their cereal or get their shoes or whatever you've asked them to do, as if they never heard a word? That might indicate that they didn't really understand; this is common among younger children, especially when given a string of directives: "Finish eating, then go upstairs and brush your teeth. While you're up there, get your shoes and bring them down, and then put on your raincoat, or we're going to be late!" Sound familiar?

• Or maybe you asked them a "why" question. Children may not know the answer to the question you ask and so don't respond, appearing not to be listening. "Why did you leave that book at child care?" is an unanswerable question. So is, "Why didn't you carry that bowl with both hands, the way I told you?"

• Another possibility is that they are faking. Maybe they are actually defying you, trying to gain control or to get you upset. And they're succeeding at the latter, aren't they? So take a look at the situations that most often end up in your getting upset. If they were only pretending not to be listening, then some feeling is behind it. Next time, try to figure out what the feeling is. Were they worried about what was going to happen at the place you were in such a hurry to get them to on time? Have the day care days not been going so swimmingly, perhaps? Were they angry at being rushed? You may not have time to discuss it right then, but later you can revisit it. Even if they can't remember, it will be helpful for them to hear you say, "You must have been upset/worried/angry. Next time you can tell me about it so you won't have to pretend you don't hear me." Then be prepared to ask and hear about that feeling next time.

• Or maybe they've learned that if they wait long enough, you'll go do it yourself. Children can be incredibly patient sometimes.

Too bad we can't have tape recordings of our voices to play back so we can hear what we sound like to our children. Sometimes we adults talk on and on, yammering away, with lectures and advice, none of which they find very helpful. One of the Grandmothers remembers giving what she thought was an informative little talk to her young son about whether he should engage in some remotely harmful activity. He waited until she was through, then asked, "Does that mean yes or no?" Would *you* listen to you?

So try saying what you need to say only once or twice, in simple terms and with few words, with the TV off and the cell phone on mute. Give them ample preparation time for each step of the early-morning routine or whatever the rushed time of day might be. And if they still don't seem to hear you, offer to listen to their reasons why not. Just don't ask them *why* they weren't listening.

We told you it was complicated!

KSB

Divorce

Dear Grandmothers,

I am a divorced mom with two kids, 6 and 9. I have the main custody of my kids, but they get time to go with their dad to his family's events during the holidays, or wherever he wants to take them.

His family hates me and tells my children bad things about me that upset the kids, and my ex does nothing to stop it—and even maybe encourages it. I can't talk to him about it.

I don't even know for sure what they say; I think my kids don't tell me when they get back because they don't want to hurt my feelings or because they are worried and confused. Or maybe they are afraid that what those people say is TRUE! What can I say to my children?

Please help,
Divorced Mom

Dear Mom,

Our hearts ache for you, they really do, because at least half of us are also Divorced Moms.

But about your kids: It seems unfair that children have to be exposed to adult conflicts when just plain growing up supplies plenty of challenges. It's so hard for kids when the people they love are in disagreement and they feel themselves being pulled apart by loyalty to both sides. To avoid this, many kids choose not to talk about it, thus avoiding additional conflict but also leaving themselves with no one to talk to about their unhappiness and confusion. Meanwhile the separated parents—consciously and subconsciously—take satisfaction in hearing recriminating things about each other, and with the relatives contributing their opinions, the children hear comments that can be unfair and exaggerated.

You have wisely decided that talking to your ex-spouse doesn't help and that you have no control over him or his family, but that what you say to your children is of primary importance. And, in fact, the Grandmothers have only three things to offer you: our empathy, hope (it may take a few years, but you will recover), and the words to say to your children:

"Daddy and I say unkind things about one another sometimes and have mean thoughts, and I know it shows. This puts you in a hard place because you love both of us. We both love you very much. Often married couples, although in love in the beginning, grow apart for many reasons. This is not your fault, even though it may feel that way sometimes, especially when you're asked to take sides. I'm going to try hard not to make you feel that way."

"It's OK to tell me how you feel about this. I know you're sometimes sad, sometimes angry, sometimes confused. I understand how mad you get at me about this, how sad it all makes you. You wish we could be one big happy family like the people you see on TV. I wish it could be different too. I'm so sorry it happened."

"When Grandma Z and Aunt Y tell you bad things about me, you have to realize that they are angry about this divorce situation, too. They feel loyalty to your dad because they've known him longer. I am sorry you have to hear those things and that they upset you. Even very nice people say mean things sometimes, especially if they are angry."

And sometimes don't say anything at all. Just listen, nod, and give your children the time and space to talk. You may hear concerns that are very different from the ones you think they're worried about.

Say the same reassuring things over and over. They need to hear them repeatedly because they will take them in at different times at different levels of understanding. Avoid asking questions; just wait for the confidences to come out gradually, when they are sure that it is safe to talk to you about their fears and concerns because you have said it is. Make it as safe for your kids as possible.

Don't try to make it better; simply acknowledge their feelings. What your children need from you is what we as adults most need when we are despondent or anxious: a willing ear, some empathic understanding, an arm around the shoulder, a hug.

It won't be easy, but you can do it.

KSB

Talking to Kids about Sex

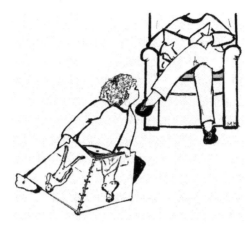

Times have changed radically since we Grannies were youngsters and able to remain naive about sexual matters until
well into our teens. But there are still some basic truths we can
pass on. They come in two varieties: timeless truths and challenging ones.

Timeless Truth No. 1: Don't tell your children more than
they ask for. When your young child sees a pregnant woman
and asks why she's so fat, tell him that she has a baby growing
inside her body, and that once *he* was a baby nestled inside
you. While you're at it, try to use the correct vocabulary. The
baby is in his mother's uterus, not her tummy. Tummies hold
food, and your child could be confused by the idea of the baby
swimming around in a sea of mashed potatoes and raisin bran.
But you can stop right there with the anatomy lesson. Save the
charts with the labeled vas deferens and fallopian tubes for the
questions that come later.

Timeless Truth No. 2: Answer the questions with matter-of-fact candor. Even if the questions make you squirm, conceal your embarrassment and don't give your child the impression that what he is asking about is ugly or unpleasant. Use the word "penis" as casually as you say "ankle" or "ear." Love and teach him love of his body uniformly. If he asks his question in a very public place, tell him that you'll talk about it later, but then be sure that you do so. To hope that he'll forget about it later is to give him the message that he's stumbled into forbidden territory. If you express alarm at what he asks, he'll stop asking.

Timeless Truth No. 3: Listen. Where do her questions come from? What has she seen or learned from a friend that is puzzling or worrying her? What does she already know that is a distortion of the truth? Children's thought processes are different from adults', and she may need your help making sense of what she's seen and heard.

Timeless Truth No. 4: Looking doesn't help, but talking does. There's a reason why the best of the books that explain procreation to children are illustrated with sweet-faced cartoon people and not photographs of adults in passionate embraces. Children would only be troubled by actual photos, and they aren't enlightened by seeing actual naked bodies, either. Their curiosity means they need to be encouraged to ask questions and have those questions answered, but with everyone calm and covered up, not excited and overstimulated.

Challenging Truth No. 1: Sexual images, conversations and even demonstrations are omnipresent. One of the reasons we Grannies were kept so innocent for so long was because then there were no adult television shows or commercials giving us gratuitous sex education lessons; even the lovers in the movies kept their clothes on in those days. Today's parents can try, but protecting children from these programs and images seems impossible; they occur at all times of the day and online everywhere. There are technological ways to keep your child from seeing adult-themed programming when your child is in her own home, but what about when she visits friends who perhaps aren't as vigilant as you are? What about the ads in magazines, newspapers, even the billboards that you drive her past on her way to preschool? And what will happen when she learns to read? Is it not also your task to prepare her for the world that she lives in, give her the information she needs to protect herself from the onslaught of sexual imagery and themes coming at her from every direction?

We won't try to come up with Challenging Truths Nos. 2–4. Challenging Truth No. 1 is quite enough. But how do you help children who have been exposed to puzzling images and words? And what if they don't ask any questions?

Watch for a telling change in his behavior. Suddenly he's popping in on you in the bathroom or bedroom, or his preschool teacher tells you he's been peeping under toilet stalls, or he's staring at you when you get undressed in a way that makes you feel uncomfortable, and it's clear that comments (or scenes on television) that used to go over his head don't any more. Or maybe he starts hanging onto his groin as if it has become risky to leave it unprotected. Any or all of these could be indications that he is puzzled and curious and is trying to understand something he's seen or heard about.

Monitor what your child sees on TV or other electronic devices, of course, and when necessary watch it with him so you can explain scenes that he might find confusing. If you're watching together and something occurs onscreen that you think might have aroused that new curiosity of his, say, "That was confusing," or "That was a surprise; what did you think was going on?" and then clarify his interpretation of the scene for him in language he can understand; lastly, invite his questions.

If he barges in on you in the shower or starts playing "doctor" with his playmates, trying to get a better view of people with their clothes off, get everyone's clothes back on (see Timeless

Truth No. 4) and say, "You must have some questions," and encourage him to ask them.

If you go to pick her up from a playdate and find her totally absorbed in a filmed sexual scene—reluctant to leave it, in fact—wait until you get her in the car but then say, "That wasn't a kids' program you were watching. Do you have some questions about it?"

For the silent types who may demonstrate concerns but don't articulate any questions, you might help them out by formulating the questions for them. You might say, "Some children have questions about shows like that one. They ask, 'Was that man hurting that woman?' Is that a question you would like to ask?" Or you might pull out that book with the sweet cartoon lovers in it to look at together, but don't be overly dependent on it. Books can never take the place of talking.

In every instance, give him (or her—we're trying to use both pronouns here) permission to ask question after question and then unflinchingly provide him/her with answer after answer. Challenging, yes. But the sooner you start, the better.

KSB

Working with Teachers

Preschool teachers and parents often greet each other at first meeting with cheerful smiles that cover up cautious, even adversarial feelings as each one sizes up the other. Will she recognize my skills and abilities, the teacher wonders, or will she be one of those nitpicky, critical mothers? What if Allison throws one of her little tizzy fits when I'm not there, the mother worries; will the teacher know how to handle it, or will she just think I'm a bad mother? And do I really trust this total stranger with my child? What if she's a screamer and an arm-squeezer, like my first-grade teacher? Or what if (the mother hardly dares consider this one) Allison ends up behaving better for her than she does for me?

Many preschool teachers and child care providers regularly attend workshops, usually called "Working with Parents," which address these concerns and focus on the goal of a partnership between parent and teacher. In these workshops teachers are encouraged to see that teacher and parents need to work together, sharing information and insights, all in the best interests of the child. Parents don't get the benefit of such workshops, but much of the advice given to teachers works equally well for parents, especially as they first enroll their children in new preschool and child care programs.

Get to know him/her. Take every advantage of the orientation period, not just to help your child adjust but to get better acquainted with your child's teacher. Put your suspicions aside and be as warm and friendly as you can, offering to help if this seems appropriate. Chat amiably during "down times" (if any) so that she can relax and not feel that you're just checking her out. Assume that partnership attitude rather than act like an employer with an employee.

Appreciate and thank her. This shouldn't be empty praise, and if your child's teacher is managing to keep a roomful of preschoolers safe and occupied, there should be a lot to admire: her creative activities, her manner with the children, her handling of the inevitable crisis situations. Teachers do not respond well to parents who approach them only to complain.

Share information with her. You needn't tell her your most intimate secrets, but anything that has happened to your child at home is worth sharing. It is just as important for the teacher to know about small triumphs (such as your child getting dressed by herself) as the early morning tantrum that might color the whole day, or the cold you think your child might be hatching. And, by all means, let your child's teacher know when major changes occur in your child's life, such as a move, a death in the family, a new baby on the way, a divorce. She can help your child cope and adjust, but only if she has been informed. Be sure to include your child in these exchanges; it will be comforting for your child to be assured that everyone knows.

Talk to your child at home about her teacher. Teachers are encouraged to speak often to the children about their parents ("You miss your mom? I know she is missing you, too"), but this is another piece of advice that goes both ways. Loyalty conflicts arise most often when a child's life seems to be divided sharply in two, home and school, with no connection between. Hang up your child's school artwork on your refrigerator, talk about the field trip her class took to the market, help her find something to bring to school to show to her teacher and the rest of the class. Most of all, let your child know that you like and approve of her teacher, and you want her to like and approve of her, too.

Be your child's advocate, but understand that your child is one of many. This is a tough one because, of course, your job is to be subjective and biased in your child's favor. But put yourself in the teacher's shoes for a minute: She has maybe 36 little mittens to keep track of, so don't berate her when at the end of the day one of your kid's is missing. Give the teacher a break and not only write your child's name on everything she brings to school but attach the mittens to the coat sleeves, the scarf to the coat collar. Save your defense of your child's rights for the times when you think her sense of well-being or even her safety is at stake. Which brings us to:

When you have a concern, voice it immediately and honestly. Don't stew silently over a supposed slight. Without accusing or judging, just stating the facts as you see them, bring it to the teacher's attention right away. If you have developed a relationship with the teacher, if you have been thanking her for the good job she has been doing and sharing home events with her as described above, she will be ready to hear your concerns and either put your mind at ease with a logical explanation or start working with you to come up with a solution to the problem.

In other words, if only for your child's sake at first, form a relationship with your child's teacher. Not only will that provide the best possible home/school adjustment for him, but chances are that over time you will find that teacher to be one of your best sources of support and encouragement as you raise your child.

But what if, after months of trying but failing to appreciate this teacher's efforts in your child's behalf, after numerous attempts at conversation that never move into the realm of friendly sharing, and, frankly, after too many instances of classroom practices about which your child complains and of which you do not approve, your relationship with your child's teacher is, if anything, strained? What then?

First of all, ask, how serious is this lack of accord between you and your child's teacher?

Does your child go to school most days happily, eagerly? Then probably you can relax. Your child's attachment to school is probably to his many friends there, not to the teacher at all. Is your issue, for instance, that your preschooler isn't being taught academics? Please realize that many educators are urging preschool teachers to put away the alphabet letters and flash cards and create an environment where children can explore, create, and enjoy being curious learners, pursuing their own interests.

And if your child does complain occasionally, what is the nature of his complaint? Try to sort out your child's perception of what happened. For example, did your child come home protesting that he didn't get to play with his new action toy that he brought to school, that in fact his teacher took it away from him? Perhaps the school policy is that toys from home are to be put safely away in cubbies so that they will not be lost or broken before day's end.

In contrast, if your child is habitually "sick" or "tired" when it is time to go to school and you sense that she is fearful of what might happen there, make it your business to observe the classroom more than once. Maybe her teacher is having difficulty managing a roomful of active children, some of whom behave in ways that can be disturbing, and your child feels unsafe, is in distress for good cause. Then, as personable as your child's teacher might be, don't dismiss your worry. Your child can sense your anxiety and adds it to her own. Now is the time to start talking to both the teacher and the preschool director about your concerns. Other children may be functioning perfectly well in this slightly chaotic atmosphere, but your child is not.

Go with your gut feeling and start considering a change of classroom or even school. There is no such thing as a one-size-fits-all teacher and classroom.

There is always the possibility, of course, that the problem is not as benign as those we have been describing here. Perhaps your child does have a difficulty that is interfering with his adjustment to school. Perhaps the teacher doesn't have the skills and maturity required to manage a classroom or relate appropriately to children and parents. Perhaps the school is saying it's the kid who has the problem while you are sure that it's the teacher who needs help. In all of these cases, the advice of an early childhood specialist is called for. Your child's school may have its own psychologist, or your pediatrician or pastor may have one to recommend.

But often such concerns are not so dramatic. Your child is neither miserable nor delighted with his preschool class, and you blow hot and cold about it as well. You have tried to form a relationship with your child's teacher, but she just isn't what you consider warm, and this worries you.

Do some observing and ask yourself a few basic questions. Is your child learning? Has he adjusted reasonably well? Consider how difficult a transition to a whole new classroom or school setting might be. Unless of course he appears to be overwhelmed, maybe in the long run it would be best to let your child remain where he is. There are lessons to be learned in less than ideal situations. This is not the only classroom he will be in that falls short of perfection. These are not the only children he will meet who have troubles. He could gain from learning how to cope, how to avoid these troubles, while learning to accept the children themselves.

Most important is to clarify what your expectations of your child's teacher are. She is not, after all, a substitute parent, but your child's teacher, maybe your child's first teacher. You are the parent, the only one whose role it is to meet your child's needs for nurturing and love. As a parent you are also a teacher, but a teacher is not a parent. Perhaps that is the place to start as you make these difficult decisions.

KSB

Kids Lost in the Holidays

It's happening again. We've all seen it before. A mother rushing along the sidewalk or through the mall, pushing a stroller and holding the hand of a 3-year-old who, in danger of having her shoulder dislocated, is half-walking, half-trotting in an effort to keep up.

The holidays are coming. The media is ratcheting up the excitement, and the stores are inviting us in with glorious decorations, repetitive holiday music and shelves overburdened with things to buy. We are beginning to feel a little overwhelmed and as though we can't keep up either. We wonder how one dictionary could ever have defined "holiday" as "That period of time when one does not work and does things for pleasure instead."

In the rush of it all, what can we do to keep the children, particularly the preschoolers, in mind over the next few weeks?

"Oh for goodness' sakes," you might say. "We constantly keep them in mind as we rush about buying them toys so they will have plenty of gifts and won't be disappointed if they don't get what the TV is urging them to ask for. We make sure they have special clothes to wear, and we hurry to get their pictures taken with Santa. What more do you want us to do?"

We Grandmothers got together and, after admitting that we, too, get caught up in holiday excitement, we decided to suggest the following ideas to young parents.

Take a minute to try to see things from young children's perspective. Perhaps your children really aren't so keen on having a picture taken with Santa. This you may observe if you stand watching preschooler after preschooler scream when lifted onto the bearded man's lap. Perhaps being pulled along through the malls trying to avoid the oncoming legs is not much fun either. On Christmas morning it's even possible that a mound of toys that one is required to open in a few hours' time is quite overwhelming.

So decide whether a picture with Santa or a trip to the mall is worth the trip, the wait and the anxiety it often causes our young children. Take a second look at that shopping list and consider shortening the part that's devoted to gifts for your kids and think about how, at this busy time, your child can actually be helpful, taking on some of the holiday tasks with an enthusiasm you lost several Decembers ago.

Kids love to help make gifts, such as cookies, and decorate butcher paper with handprints or potato prints to use as wrapping paper. Any mess can be cleaned up faster than you can go to a mall, find a parking space, lift your preschooler out of his car seat and keep track of him as you run from store to store. More importantly, the times you are quietly spending with your child and the inner pleasure she feels as she makes the gift, gives it, and is showered with appreciation far outweighs the time it takes to clean up.

When your holiday involves travel to visit a friend or relative, prepare your children for what will happen. We take so
many things for granted and forget it is all new to them. They
may erroneously think, as one Grandmother's grandchild did,
that they won't be returning home.

Young children fill in missing information with their own
private assumptions, often not voiced because they are afraid
of what they may hear. "Where will I sleep? Is there a bathroom there? What's a kennel and what will happen to Spot?
Will someone feed him? Will we ever see him again?"

Or maybe you are going to be the hosts instead of the guests
and household members will be shifted to other rooms to make
room for grandparents or friends. A discussion with your preschooler ahead of time about where everyone will sleep and for
how long can help alleviate anxiety. Being included in the planning and learning about hospitality enriches the experience in
ways that live well beyond these holidays.

In other words, let's reduce the times when mothers are feeling they have to rush along, dragging their children behind
them as they try to get it all done. Make these holidays "those
periods of time when one does not work and does things for
pleasure instead."

MLK

Kid Likes Daddy Better

Dear Grandmothers,

Lately our 2-year-old daughter has been rejecting me in favor of her father. She wants Daddy to read her a bedtime story, Daddy to pour her juice, Daddy to hold her hand, etc. I know I shouldn't let it get to me, but it does. Any advice?

—Rejected Mom

Dear Rejected,

If trying not to let it get to you isn't working, you might want to consider possible reasons why your daughter has started choosing Daddy instead of Mommy. We're not suggesting, nor do we think that you are, that you wouldn't want her to love being with her daddy. We're only responding to your feeling of being left out. So we're suggesting a few possibilities:

She's 2 years old. Two-year-olds are newly aware of their independence and want to demonstrate it, insist upon it, make every one of the decisions open to them and even a few that aren't. They also love to tease. Is there a mischievous little twinkle in her eye when she asks for Daddy, not you, to tie her shoe?

She wants to be in control. That also comes with being two and isn't likely to go away when she turns three. What better way to gain control of her parents than to have them vying for the privilege of tucking her in bed at night?

She is angry at you for making her feel left out, so she's going to make *you* feel left out. You leave her all day at the child care center, you brought home that baby brother that you're fussing over all the time, and you sometimes go out with Daddy in the evening and make her stay home with a sitter, just to name a few of your crimes.

She's learning to try out her preferences—in fact, she's just beginning to learn that she *has* preferences. She's experimenting with choosing what food she wants to eat, what clothes she wants to wear, and even with what parent she wants to buckle her into her car seat.

If this I-want-Daddy-not-you behavior persists and it's still getting to you, you might want to start talking to her about it. Try saying something like, "Sounds like you want Mommy to feel left out. I'll be happy when you start choosing me again for some of the things that you need to have done." Daddy might also tell her that he doesn't think it's fun if Mommy never gets a turn. And if she becomes altogether too dictatorial, it's time for both parents to step in and let her know that she may think she wants to be the boss, but that really you and Daddy are. If bedtime has become the issue, for example, come up with a schedule: Mondays, Wednesdays and Fridays are Daddy's nights to read the bedtime story, but Tuesdays, Thursdays and Saturdays are Mommy's. It's not an option anymore. On Sundays, *she* can decide.

Our guess is that by the time the second Sunday rolls around, she will have forgotten about her previous preferences and start choosing Mommy just as often as she chooses Daddy.

KSB

Adoption

The first thing you need to know about adopted children is that, just as with all children, they each traverse their own particular path and, for the most part, they turn into happy, well-adjusted adults.

The second thing you need to know is that, just as with all children, the chances that adopted children will turn into happy, well-adjusted adults can be greatly increased if you are attentive to their feelings and questions and are honest in your responses. This means you also have to be attentive to your own feelings and honest with yourself—and sometimes this is the harder of the two.

Parents come to adoption with an array of feelings, some more evident than others: elation, hope, anxiety, even sadness. They may carry feelings about not having been able to have their own child, about the challenges the process of adoption entailed, and often about the suddenness of the actual adoption, which did not provide them the usual nine months to prepare. Then, too, there are delights and disappointments when the actual child arrives. It is never exactly as expected. All these feelings may be experienced as transient; after a while parents' feelings about parenting the actual child with whom they have established a parental "forever" relationship supersede the earlier feelings. At times, however, the feelings creep back in, perhaps creating more guilt or irritation than necessary. This impacts parenting, which impacts the child. For this reason, it's important to be aware of the many feelings that may be at play and process them. Some parents need to allow themselves to mourn the loss of their own biological child in order to be sufficiently open to their adopted child; some need to be up front with themselves about their feelings regarding the biological parent in order to protect their child from the more subtle negative inferences the child might pick up; some need to be kind to themselves and recognize that their supposed failures to connect at the beginning could be related to the fact they had no time to prepare for the child's arrival.

The circumstances of the adoption can range from a well-planned, relatively smooth experience of a carefully chosen brand new infant to a harrowing number of years waiting and then struggling with foreign government bureaucracies and the archaic procedures of impoverished orphanages in order to finally bring a now-older child home. These circumstances make a significant difference for the child as well as the parent. The more a parent is prepared for the hardships and complications, the better they'll be able to focus on the child's experience at transition time and in the aftermath. For local adoptions this can simply mean having someone to talk to about your worry that the biological parent will change her mind—so that you can free yourself up to bond with the new baby. For older children it can mean preparing yourself for the fact that the child will be going through a difficult separation and that your love alone might not make it instantly all better.

Helping your child with the knowledge that they've been

adopted is an ongoing process, never finished. It inevitably becomes (or is) part of their sense of themselves and can't be avoided. Just keep in mind that this is not a bad thing and that, though your child might have painful feelings associated with the adoption, it's just like everything else: Children bring many feelings of all sorts to their relationship with you. All children have feelings and fantasies about their parents, themselves, and their circumstances; some are positive and some are not so positive. What makes a difference is the degree to which children's feelings are listened to, questions are answered, and incorrect ideas are dispelled. Protecting a child from the knowledge of the adoption might feel like a kind thing at the time, but in the long run, it can hurt more. At the same time, giving a child too much knowledge, information he or she is not yet ready to process, may be overwhelming. For this reason, many parents choose to talk about the adoption from the beginning in a matter-of-fact, nondetailed way, and then listen to and respond to the child's questions as they arise. If you have an open, communicative relationship with your child, then the child will let you know when he or she is ready for the next conversation and clarification.

Children develop their identities in stages as they grow. Initially a child's identity is inextricably entwined with the parent(s) and the security they provide. An infant feels like "a someone" in the context of a caring, continuous relationship. Children adopted at a later age have had a previous relationship with an adult, whether biological parent, foster parent, or child-care giver, and are inextricably connected to "the someone" that they are. This relationship is part of their identity and needs to be considered when the adoption occurs and when subsequently talking about it. (For parents to know: Generally, the better the relationship a child has had with their first caregiver, the better they'll be able to make a relationship with the adoptive parents.) There is a disruption that occurs at the time of the adoption, and it helps a child to have something from their previous life, whether a soft toy or a piece of clothing, that they can hold on to as a reminder of that part of themselves that, in a way, was lost.

We all construct life narratives in our minds, often continuously revised, and these invariably include our understanding of our origins. Adopted children's narratives can have holes that they fill with their own fantasies until the reality of their story is gradually pieced together with clarifications and information they are ready to hear. Parents can help with this by having a visual narrative to help link their child's early experience with their current existence. Many adoptive parents take photographs of the child's circumstances at the time of the adoption, including pictures of the orphanage and/or caregivers, and place them in an album so they can share them with their child when he is ready.

Toddlers and preschoolers need to know that they are loved, will be kept safe, and that they've got the right equipment to make it in the world. This is a time when a child needs some kind of explanation related to the reasons he was adopted and reassurance that he is loved by you, that you are his forever Mommy and Daddy, and, if appropriate, that his birth mommy loved him very much but couldn't take care of him. (When this isn't the case, there may be other ways to bring out a positive side, and, if not, eventually ways to feel sad together about the earlier tragedy.) Older preschoolers are often curious about where they came from and observant of pregnant mothers and babies. A child can make a casual reference to "when I was in your body, Mommy . . ." cueing you in to the need to explain that in fact he came from another woman's uterus. He might feel upset by this for awhile, "but I want to have come from your body, Mommy (just like my sister)" and may need to be allowed and supported in mourning the wished-for impossibility. You might have this sadness, too, and can share it with him. The ability to feel sad about something that can't be changed is a life skill that builds resiliency.

Families who have adopted children of a different nationality or race often feel it is important to support the child by introducing her to her cultural heritage, sometimes providing language lessons, sometimes making trips to the country from whence she came. This is confusing to young children, whose identities are so wrapped up in their parents and whose cognitive capacities aren't yet developed enough to make sense of the bigger world. It can be of interest to school-age children, however, who are ready and able to learn about the world beyond themselves, and who may have concerns about their differences. They can take advantage of such cultural experiences best when they themselves choose to engage in them—more so than when it's the parents' choice. This is always true but especially so when the child might take it the wrong way from the parent. He could add to his fantasies the idea that the parents will only like him if he fits their idea of who he is.

Adolescents are actively seeking out their identities as separate from their parents, often looking for role models outside the home. It is during adolescence, then, that some adoptive children begin to think in more detail about their origins and have a wish to seek out their biological parent. For others, this wish happens during adulthood, but it's not inevitable that an adopted person will want to do this. Some say they really have no interest since their adoptive parents are their real parents.

At times, the multitude of variables impacting adopted children and their parents, including the child's inner perceptions of his circumstances, make it difficult for the child to sort out his concerns, even with parental help. In such situations, there are skilled professionals available to help you and/or your child explore the reasons for his and your feelings and difficulties.

BUS

Being a Parent Is Even Harder These Days

Maybe Grandmothers of every age have looked around at what this world is coming to, sighed, and told each other that the upcoming generation is in trouble. We do worry about you young parents, who have decisions to make about your small children that we never had, decisions with serious consequences—starting with deciding to have children in the first place. We didn't decide to have kids; they just appeared. And we didn't think we had to have the best baby equipment, the best toys, the best classes and playmates and playtimes and safety gear for our children—we just let them make mud pies and then scrubbed them off, piled them all in the back of our station wagons (no car seats, no safety belts) and drove them to the five and dime store for candy. Most of us mothers had the luxury of staying home with our kids at least until they were school age. And we didn't read books about, or worry about, our children's fragile egos or bleak-appearing futures.

We're glad that you read books and that you're reading this one. But we're pretty sure that we're telling you what you already know.

Let Them Play

Research has vindicated the mothers of half a century ago who routinely opened the back screen door and told their kids to go play, and not to bother coming back until the streetlights came on or they heard the dinner bell. Turns out these mothers were not being abusive and neglectful. The moms of the previous century didn't know it, of course, but they were ensuring that their children developed a critical cognitive skill called "executive function."

Before kids' hours were filled with TV, video games and electronic toys—or yoga classes, soccer games and tiny-tot gymnastics—they regulated their own activities, mostly in improvised, imaginative play. They played "cops and robbers," "house," or "school," their own reality-based dramas. They also became the characters in fantasies involving queens and dragons, cowboys and horses, flying caped heroes and tall buildings, pirates and sinking ships. And as they did this, researchers are telling us now, they were developing executive function, the ability to self-regulate, which turns out to be a better indicator of success in school than the results of an IQ test. Kids with good self-regulation skills are better able to control their emotions and resist impulsive behavior.

Those were different times, of course, and there's no going back to them. Kicking one's kids out of the house is no longer considered good form. And kids shooed outside into a modern-day subdivision would probably come home bored anyway because there wouldn't be any other kids out there for them to play with. Those kids are inside their house, bickering over which channel to watch, perhaps, or gobbling down a quick supper so they won't be late for Tee-Ball practice.

There are a couple of reasons for this shift. First of all, we now seem to be afraid to permit our children to play unsupervised. We fear child molesters and imagine all sorts of accidents that could befall them. In vain do statisticians tell us that our children's chances of being molested are no greater than they ever were, and that accidents are even more rare. And secondly, we now feel that we have to give our children every possible opportunity to add to their repertoire of skills. How can he become a musical prodigy if he doesn't attend toddler Suzuki classes? How can she become a soccer star if she doesn't join the team as soon as she can walk? If we don't make sure our kids have these opportunities, they'll be at a disadvantage compared to all the other children who are on all the right teams, in all the best classes.

So, how do we reconcile today's anxious parents and the highly structured environment with our children's need for unstructured, self-regulated play?

Let's start with the givens: We're not going to cancel all his classes and sports activities, and we're not going to let him play totally unsupervised. But we can certainly limit the number of teams and classes we sign him up for.

Very young children don't need anything extra outside of the occasional play date, if that. Toddlers might enjoy an hour or so per week at a class designed for kids their age where they can run and move freely, either to music or on gymnastics mats and 6-inch-high balance beams, but no more. Older preschoolers would probably benefit from regularly attending a preschool where the bulk of time is given over to free play. A kindergartener might join a soccer team where cooperation, not competition, is stressed, but only if he expressed interest. The primary requirement for unsupervised play is uninterrupted stretches of time, and we could certainly cut back on all those classes and practices in order to give our children a little more of it.

And while we're not going to let our children play entirely unsupervised, we don't need to be hovering over them either. Even the youngest children are quite capable of entertaining, even educating, themselves. We can stay nearby, assuring ourselves that we are keeping them safe, but at the same time go about our own business and not intervene unless it becomes quite clear that we're needed. We can limit TV and other screen time to an hour a day, tops, and start buying our children uncomplicated toys—and fewer of them. We can encourage complex imaginative play by offering simple props and play ideas but then withdraw so the children can plan their own scenarios and act them out. Even the smallest toddler, given the opportunity, will start feeding the baby or driving his car down the highway. Older children will become family members, characters from stories, powerful heroes, animals in the jungle, royalty, all the while devising plotlines and scene changes worthy of the most skilled dramatist.

Imagine your children, along with those of your more enlightened friends, enjoying whole afternoons of such brain-enriching, creative play. Then imagine your snoopy neighbor observing them and starting to brag about how her 3-year-old excels in karate, chess and ballroom dancing. You needn't be intimidated. You can tell her that your 3-year-old, who appears to be feeding dryer lint to her teddy bear, is actually improving her executive function. Your neighbor will surely be impressed. And you will be confident that your child is spending precious time at the activity that children need most and love best: independent, imaginative play.

KSB

Disrespect

"We'd like to have our children visit us, but I have to admit, we wish they wouldn't bring their little kids with them," a grandfather remarked. It seems he had been visited by his children and grandchildren and was still reeling from the event. He complained, "They never listened, interrupted, didn't want to do anything, were picky about the food and got into arguments about toys. Today, I guess kids are like that."

This grandfather's tirade was not unfamiliar to The Grandmothers who have noticed some young children complaining, yelling at adults, insisting on having their favorite foods, and apparently requiring constant entertainment. How, one wonders, did the parents feel during that visit, and what did the children take away with them? Perhaps they picked up their grandfather's impatience and even the subtle, or maybe not so subtle, message that they were not necessarily well-liked.

Parents today are very aware of children's needs and often

bend over backwards to understand and pay attention to them. They sacrifice themselves to be sure their children have a variety of experiences, and participation in their many activities is taken for granted.

The idea that children should be seen and not heard has gone by the wayside. However, while working hard to make the world a child-friendly place, adults have often allowed it to become child-dominated.

Children learn respect and appreciation for others by having those responsible for them appreciate and respect them. They absorb ways to behave not only from the behavior of those around them but also through the parental coaching they experience from their early years through adulthood.

Consideration for and noticing others have become increasingly difficult because adults and young children have become so distracted by technology. Helping children notice others is so often forgotten. The Grandmothers think a few examples might help.

A young mother and her 3-year-old daughter were visiting friends for lunch. As the peanut butter and jelly sandwiches were put on the table, Sarah loudly exclaimed, "That's chunky peanut butter! I don't like chunky peanut butter. I only like creamy peanut butter!" To some, such assertiveness seems rude. To others, it's admirable for Sarah to stand up for what she likes and dislikes.

This is an opportunity for Sarah's mother to suggest there are others to be considered. She might quietly coach her daughter by saying, "Mrs. Smith made these sandwiches especially for our lunch. Could you try one?" When Sarah loudly says, "No" (and chances are she will), settling for a glass of milk would be just fine. It's better for this little girl to learn to think about another person than to watch the hostess hurry to prepare a separate lunch. A missed lunch won't harm her, and she can be quietly reassured she can have a snack when she gets home.

In this situation Sarah can observe her mother's behavior, hear her words and the tone she uses, feel her respect for their hostess, and experience Mom's acknowledgment that at this point in her life Sarah prefers smooth peanut butter.

As parents struggle through the challenge of socializing their kids, teaching the idea of sharing can be problematic. Parents who take pride in assertiveness may well be distressed when little Sean screams at his friend Jason for playing with his favorite truck. The more talk there is about sharing, the louder Sean protests until we have two crying 3-year-olds on our hands.

To try to avoid these meltdowns, preparation before an upcoming visit is a good idea. Talking about what's ahead doesn't necessarily work with toddlers, but a parent can begin the business of socializing Sean with something like, "Jason is coming. He likes trucks, so let's make sure we have two trucks to play with."

Now a fair warning has been given. If Jason again grabs that favorite truck, be prepared. Sean may scream in protest. Instead of demanding that he share the toy or sending him to his room, calmly move in, acknowledge the fact that they both like trucks, and distract them with other attractive toys. This is respectful of how each toddler feels because at this stage in their development they can only see things from their own point of view. How others feel is not yet within their understanding. A parent's approach to this is so important. Kids will absorb a calm demeanor, hear the words used and gradually learn to share.

As Sean turns three or four and can remember times when he and Jason have played together, prepare him for an upcoming visit. Respecting his attachment to a toy, you can say, "Jason and his mom are coming over this afternoon. I know it's hard for you to let him play with that special truck. Can he play with it this time, or should we put it away?"

This respects how attached he is to the toy and gives him

some control over what will happen. Chances are it will go better this time, and then his kindness can be acknowledged.

How parents listen to children is essential if they expect to be listened to and respected. When talking with a child, try to ignore a ringing phone. Calls can be returned later; continuing the conversation gives the message that what is being said is important. Remember, children are watching when a parent's ringing phone has to be answered even though it interrupts an in-person conversation with a friend. Children hear and imitate everything!

Consider times adult guests are visiting and kids burst into the room in the full bloom of an argument demanding that it be settled—*now!* It helps everyone when parents quietly excuse themselves and find a private place to talk, rather than embarrass everyone by flooding the room with anger and demeaning words. This is respectful of the guests and the children alike. It models for them how and when to talk about conflicts and where to do it in the most appropriate ways.

Children can be gently coached not to interrupt or at least to say, "Excuse me," when something is urgent. Kids will gradually learn to wait when adults are having conversations just as parents, in turn, will wait until after their friends have left to discuss potentially embarrassing issues with their children.

All this is not easy. Popular movies and TV shows feature kids with quick, smart-sounding back talk, directed not just at peers but adults as well. While watching these with young children, point out that what is done on the screen isn't always kind and respectful of others. Talk about how we might all feel if someone talked to us in those words. Parents today have to work harder to overcome the meanness seen and heard all around us.

If the process of coaching begins in the early years, then, as the children mature, they will be able to notice others, listen when people are talking and contribute to a more civil society.

Then perhaps that grandfather will tell his friends, "We love having our kids come for a visit, especially when they bring our wonderful grandchildren with them."

MLK

Stop Entertaining

"Entertainers" are what we call those parents, and many adults in young children's lives, who seem compelled to pack children's days with constant fun and exciting learning experiences. For these parents, a 4-year-old's birthday party can't be a laid-back affair with a few guests; it has to be a trip to a Broadway play or local carnival. These parents worry that because there is so much to learn, their children must be stimulated in innovative ways 24/7 or they'll never make it in our fast-paced world.

Many of us fall into this trap. The problem is that constantly entertaining is exhausting. Parents may come to feel a little annoyed by always having to dream up new activities and may even be stressed by it all. We dare not admit it, however! But the truth is, children need some time to themselves, just like adults—time to mull over things they have done and ideas that have grown from earlier experiences.

We hear kids say, "I'm so bored!" We Grandmothers believe

that being bored from time to time can inspire a child's ability to invent or create. Often that "in-between" time actually stimulates new ideas, new thinking and new ways for children to become engaged and imagine activities all on their own. Never allowing children to be bored denies them the time to invent ways to fill in that time and to creatively make use of earlier experiences. This is the kind of learning that is often remembered because it satisfies and builds toward more complicated thinking. A little boredom and restlessness is good for them, for all of us.

Children love to learn. They explore, ask questions, watch everything that adults do and imitate them. They don't mind if something doesn't make sense or work out the first time—it's all a work in process. A toddler repeatedly turns a door handle or flips a light switch; a preschooler pours and re-pours water from a pitcher or hammers a nail in a log; a child throws balls into a basket in the yard—no child needs an adult guiding and correcting their every move. On the contrary, they are learning that perseverance leads to mastery. It turns out learning to tolerate making mistakes the first time we try something is an important step in development. Making a mistake, we gradually learn, isn't the end of the world; it's important for children to practice and then to move forward as mistakes are made.

When parents repeatedly step in to fix, guide and entertain their kids, they begin to create a dependency. Children will eventually look for an adult to determine what activity will be next, what will work and what won't. They learn to expect compliments and applause, regardless of effort. And worst of all, they are deprived of the satisfaction of persevering and accomplishing something by themselves. That feeling is a reward all on its own, and it's from this kind of learning that self-esteem takes root and grows.

Ask any adult to recall occasions from childhood when they felt really good about doing something, and nine times out of

10 it will be something they achieved with little or no adult assistance. Remember this when you're watching a child wobbling down the sidewalk on a two-wheeler without training wheels, or a toddler struggling to climb the stairs, or the preschooler who finally ties her shoe by herself.

Children are wired to move and think and learn on their own. In parents' eagerness to be the best, most responsible and loving parents, they can encourage their children without being entertainers. They can physically and emotionally provide safe, rich environments and demonstrate confidence in their children's innate abilities, enthusiasm, energy and curiosity. Taking comfort in knowing that their children's own abilities to discover, learn and master new things on their own will be one of the best and most long-lasting rewards—not only for the children but for the parents.

MLK

The Invasion of Technology

Parents today face challenges we Grandmothers never imagined back when we were raising children—the most obvious being the invasion of technology into virtually every aspect of life. While we're delighted to have long-distance conversations with our grandchildren via a video chat and appreciate the convenience of cell phones and texting, we know that for parents of young children, the barrage of media is an overwhelming force and something with which they must do constant battle.

Much has been written about the adverse effects of TV, video games, Internet, cell phones and tablets. Overuse of these devices is not good for children, if only because the hours they spend looking at screens have taken the place of many important things kids used to do. Talking to and connecting with other people, playing with toys and games, going outside and being physically active may seem like simple activities, but each of them is quite powerful in fostering children's physical, intellectual and social development.

Technology also impacts children indirectly through their parents. When Mommy and Daddy are so focused on their devices that they can't give their full attention to their baby, there is a lack of the attachment that the baby craves and that helps her become a full human being. When parents are always distracted by their cell phones, children may begin turning to technology as a more reliable object of attachment than the human beings in their lives.

A parent's overfocus on the phone or Internet also has a negative impact on a child's behavior. We Grandmothers remember how our kids would invariably act up and get into trouble when we spent too much time talking on the phone. But with the ubiquity of devices today and the addictiveness of platforms like Facebook, Instagram and Twitter, the pulls on parents' attention are multiplied many times over. And the kids' bad behavior multiplies as well.

To prevent the creep of tech dependency into your family life—and to make sure you don't lose your kids forever to the digital world when they become teenagers—it is important to take steps now in their earliest years. Here are some suggestions for making this happen:

First, become aware of how much time you yourself are spending with your devices. If this is a problem, acknowledge it. Set aside certain times of the day for checking emails and browsing social media, and try to ignore your devices at other times. When you are with your child, give her your full attention, look at her and show her that you care about what she has to say.

Avoid exposing babies and toddlers younger than 18 months to social media, or only allow it when a parent is on hand to share the experience, interpret it and talk about it with her.

Resist the temptation to hand your child a device to distract him when he is upset, as doing so will only create a dependency. Kids must learn to comfort themselves, and it's the parents' job to help them do this. Of course, it's easier to quiet a fretful child with colorful cartoons and cheery sounds on the iPad, but this lays the groundwork for big troubles to come—

temper tantrums when he wants the device and can't have it and an inability to tolerate and cope with difficult feelings. It's easier to avoid opening the door to this bad habit now than having to break it later when it is firmly entrenched.

For children between the ages of 18 months and 5 years, limit time on social media to one hour a day and then only with a parent present. If it helps you to get the dinner on the table, a preschooler-appropriate movie or game on the tablet could be OK, but that's all. Just be sure you've programmed the device to shut off once the story is over, not go directly to another one and hooking your child into watching more and more.

Turn off the TV when no one is watching.

Use the iPad as you would a picture book, looking at it along with your child and talking with her about the pictures and story.

Make the hour before bedtime totally media-free. The blue light from the computer monitor and cell phone screens inhibits melatonin production and interferes with sleep.

Keep a box in the dining room where all members of the family can stash their silenced phones during mealtimes.

Keep another box in the car for holding silenced devices on the ride to child care or preschool. Think of all the good conversations you'll be able to have once the kids' phones are turned off.

Consider substituting music, podcasts, and audiobooks for TV and iPad. Kids' brains are more active when they listen to a story and have to visualize what they're hearing. Once their eyes lock on to a TV or iPad screen, the brain tends to go into a passive mode where learning is at a minimum.

If your child is already dependent on her device, don't just take it away from her cold turkey because she won't know what to do instead. Help her learn to play with toys and games by playing alongside her for a while, then gradually phasing yourself out of the picture.

Add more people-centered, physical activities to your family's repertoire: establish a weekly game night, take hikes in the woods, visit neighborhood playgrounds. In this way you will make sure that the whole family is having a more balanced and well-rounded life, of which moderate, healthy media use is but one part.

GTR

Too Many Toys

When playing with friends during your early years, do you remember arranging big leaf dishes and acorn cap cups on an old tree stump to have a tea party with dolls as guests? Did you stir up dandelion leaves with grass, weave the stems and blossoms into crowns, or split the stem ends with your fingers, twisting them to make curl? We Grandmothers remember those times.

We Grandmothers don't remember a home chock full of toys. We don't remember dining-room floors or living-room chairs heaped with talking dolls, cars that beep and countless educational games.

We bring this up because a friend of ours complained the other day about not being able to walk across the floor or find a place to sit down on a friendly visit to a neighbor's home. My friend went on to describe how uncomfortable it was, during the entire visit, to watch her neighbor pick everything up all the while nagging her 4-year-old to help.

How did we go from a few toys to rooms full of stuff? We know parents are eager for their kids to have everything advertisers promise—especially when those promises include academic success. We Grandmothers admit to getting caught up in all that advertisers promise, too. But the question should not be, "Will my kid get into Harvard by playing with all these toys?" but rather, "Are more toys the answer to supporting their developing brains, emerging curiosity and creativity, sociability and physical adeptness?"

And we need to ask a second question: "How do the children themselves actually perceive the house full of toys?"

We know that the world has dramatically changed since we Grandmothers were young preschoolers. The toy business has ballooned, and advertisers have taken over. Toy companies can employ designers who are paid to carefully observe young children at play, see what they find to play with and the ways they are being imaginative and creative. Even the most spontaneous, mundane play activity observed is now developed into an expensive toy in a big box aimed at parents eager to buy the items stamped with the "educational" label.

The sobering fact is that play itself is truly educational when the child uses his imagination and brain as he plays. His sense of self is nurtured as he decides how to fashion things with "found" materials or simple toys, such as blocks, dolls and even cardboard boxes. He can give inanimate objects life, names, words and movement. He can change the attributes of the things with which he plays without the restraints of rules or adults who know how toys should be used. He perseveres, deals with frustration and works things out as he and his friends negotiate next steps together. Quarrels over toy ownership are then reduced. Homes remain relatively uncluttered.

When toys are spilling out into the common areas of the home, even the youngest members of the family can feel overwhelmed by the mess and by the number of choices. In addition, a young child's understanding of the world may become quite self-centered if parents let her spread her things through-out the house, oblivious of others who live there. It is in these early years that we need to help children develop respect for the things that surround them and begin to develop the social skills needed to be aware of others. Caring for our belongings and being aware of others is part of growing up.

We have been so focused these days on making sure that our children have every opportunity that we begin to trust the advertisers and their messages and mistrust our own common sense. Worse than that, we often ignore or are unaware of a child's ability to entertain herself and fail to recognize her innate curiosity and creative drive.

We are not suggesting children never be given toys or that everything children use should be kept out of sight. We are sug-gesting "toys in moderation." More innovative play and prob-lem-solving abilities result when there are fewer toys to distract children's imaginations. So much is learned when they create their own play alone or with friends, and it will be so much more relaxing for everyone if that adult, at the end of a working day, is able to sit down and relax in a toy-free chair.

MLK

PART TWO

Being a Child Is Hard

Kids are Not Short Adults

Children don't think the way we do, nor perceive reality in the same way. Their reality is in fact very different from ours. Obviously we can't read their minds, but we can certainly disabuse ourselves of the notion that they are being difficult just to annoy us. Most of us can't remember our thought processes when we were small children so are amazed to discover that, for example, a young child absolutely believes that people in costumes really are who they appear to be. Read on.

Separations

One of the Grandmothers' biggest challenges when we were employed as directors of child care centers was to convince the parents how important they were to their children. Always harried and hurried, these young moms and dads sometimes actually believed that their kids were happier when they were in their teachers' care than when they were with their families. And they were half afraid that their children were more fond of their teacher than they were of them.

We are here to assure you that your children don't like their teacher or other caregiver more than they like you. They will never like or need their teacher or anyone else with the enormous love and attachment they feel for you. Therefore, we don't want you to feel overwhelming guilt for leaving them with a sitter or in a child care center. We want instead for you to realize not only how important you are to them but that how you handle your separations from them is one of your most important tasks as a parent. Starting with the first time they whisk your baby off to the hospital nursery, followed by your first day back to work, your first babysitter, the first child care center or preschool, the first kindergarten class, and on and on, until way too soon you're searching for a tissue because you're being separated by a high school graduation. You know how hard those separations can be for you. Try to imagine what they mean for your young child, who doesn't understand time and so doesn't know for sure that you're ever coming back.

What makes it worse is that every one of those separations will lead to new situations with new relationships to adjust to, involving more separations. You agree that it can be hard to leave your baby with a brand new early childhood teacher, right? Just wait until you have to say goodbye to that same beloved teacher in a year or two! And how wonderful that she has become beloved, almost a member of the family, who realizes how important you are to your child and daily helps him keep you in mind.

So maybe you've got a little one who rolls with the punches and seems to be able to say goodbye with scarcely a backward glance. Don't think for a minute that those separations aren't hard for that child. You're actually lucky if you have a sobber and a clinger, a kid who reminds you every time how tough it can be to say goodbye. Children grow up saying goodbye over and over again. But parents can help by acknowledging how tough separations can be and finding ways to manage those goodbyes. Your young children are brand new to this world and need guidance.

In fact, virtually every challenge that parents and their young children face starts with your being separated from one another. You can prepare for separations and talk about them, but by all means don't do all the talking. Watch for different behaviors, listen for their thoughts and feelings, for their sadness but also their pride in getting bigger, learning to do big-kid things.

KSB

Children's Stress

Dear Grandmothers,

Lately my daughter has been waking up almost every night with terrible nightmares. It's hard to get her to get to sleep in the first place, and then when she wakes up with these bad dreams she's up for the rest of the night. My sister says this is a sign of stress. How could this be? She's only 5 years old. And if it is stress, is there a way parents can help their children handle it so they (and everyone else) can get some sleep?
—Tired Mom

Dear Tired Mom,

Children experience stress much as adults do. How they show it varies with age: An infant may cry all the time or vomit excessively; an older child may whine, misbehave, tease or have sleeping difficulties and nightmares as your daughter does; others may start wetting the bed again or appear hyperactive; school-age children may develop difficulties with peers or school work. Sometimes stress in children is evidenced physically as it is in adults with headaches, stomach aches, irritability and unusual tiredness.

With our very serious adult worries about money, jobs and difficult relationships, it is hard for us to imagine how a child who appears to have no responsibilities and nothing to do but play all day could possibly be experiencing stress. But children can become quite anxious over any number of situations, all the more when they don't quite understand them. They can somehow feel the stress of their parents even when we do all we can to shield them from our anxiety.

Which brings up what might be a major cause of our adult stress: the environment, the economy, political unrest, terrorism, mass shootings, the threat of nuclear war—all of the very serious issues that we hear, read and watch daily on the news. One easy solution to this stressor is to turn it off until she's safely in bed. She doesn't need to hear our shouting back at the politician we disagree with or responding with hand-wringing alarm to the most recent disaster. But if she does hear about these concerns, we can assure her that there are wise adults in charge (even if we privately can only hope so), and they are taking good care of our city, our country, our planet. Just as we, her parents, are taking good care of her.

If we are experiencing some household stress of which he could not help but be aware, we can share with the child what's going on. What we say depends upon the child's age, of course, but better to explain the problem as an adult concern—something that the grown-ups will handle and that he needn't worry about—than to leave him thinking that whatever has caused his parents to get upset is his fault.

We can refrain from having conversations that a child might misinterpret in front of the child. For example, a child might overhear her mother saying on the phone, "I can't stand it anymore—she is driving me crazy—for two cents I'd just up and leave!" and become terrified that Mom is going to leave home when in reality Mom is talking about a work situation.

We can examine our own hard-won ability to manage stress.

If our child is likely to "catch" our stress from us, then we need to look at the ways we cope in stressful situations and perhaps find more helpful solutions. We also need to model effective stress-management strategies for our children.

Children have very real worries of their own. We parents want so much to believe that our children are happy and care-free that we forget how painful rejection by a playmate once felt, how terribly frightened we once were of dogs or kidnappers or the class bully. We need to listen closely and carefully when our children tell us about their anxieties and offer help when that is possible. We want to take what they tell us seriously, never find ourselves dismissing what they tell us as insignificant.

Whenever possible, we can prepare our child for upcoming stressful events. Whether it's the start of school, a move into a new home or a visit to the doctor, it's always a good idea to spend some time with the child to discuss what will be happening. In many cases, the parent and child can decide in advance how the child can cope should she feel anxious, scared or nervous. Some suggestions: Tell Mom or Dad how they are feeling; count to ten; find a quiet corner and read a book; say to someone, "I need a hug!"

Perhaps more importantly, we can always be supportive and empathic about our children's worries. However trivial the child's concern may seem to us, it is serious to the child. A child under stress needs more than the usual amount of warmth and closeness, just as we do.

During times of stress, we may want to find time to just sit and be together with our child: to chat or read a book, take a walk or relax quietly in the park or the back yard. Often just an extra smile, a hug or some quiet words of praise can be the kind of therapy needed to help a child manage day-to-day stresses.

KSB

Baby and Toddler Fears

Baby Emma is so different now. As a newborn she beamed happily when she was passed around among admiring aunts and cousins. But now, at seven months, she protests loudly when anyone unfamiliar picks her up and will only tolerate being held by her mother. Going to the babysitter's house has also become a problem. Emma's parents wonder what has happened to their good-natured, even-tempered little one.

Two-year-old Ryan never even noticed the vacuum cleaner or the garbage truck before, but now he covers his ears and runs out of the room at every loud noise. He's also terrified he might go down the drain along with the bath water and believes there is a monster under his bed. His parents worry that he will be a fearful sissy all his life if they don't toughen him up right now.

Jack has been running erratically around the house and is no longer able to play with other children without chasing and scaring them. Could this have something to do with that movie he keeps asking to watch over and over?

All these are examples of typical baby and toddler fears that parents and caregivers will surely recognize. But it isn't just the child who cries and looks afraid who is fearful. It's also children who act silly, who bite their nails or suck their thumbs excessively, who insist they're not afraid, and whose eating and sleeping patterns change dramatically. Parents need to be detectives, on the lookout for fears that may underlie erratic or unusual behaviors.

Some fears make sense to parents—like big dogs and the sudden or loud noises of things, like thunder and self-flushing toilets in public places, which really can startle a young child or hurt his extra-sensitive ears. However, there are other fears that don't make obvious sense—irrational fears, which parents may dismiss or become annoyed or angry about.

Let's take a closer look at the scenarios described above. In her unhappiness, Baby Emma is showing us that she is now able to tell the difference between Mom and other less essential people. It will take time and growth for her to understand that, when Mommy goes away, she always comes back, and in the meantime other friendly people can be a pleasant substitute.

Ryan is also taking a further step in understanding the world when he notices that water disappears down the bathtub drain. But because he has not yet reached the stage of cognitive development when he can judge the relative size of things, he doesn't realize that he, too, won't get swept away along with the water. And aside from the fact that they hurt his ears, loud noises also may scare him because he assumes the trucks and vacuum cleaners that make all that noise must harbor some pretty big, unmanageable feelings, similar to what he feels when he is mad at Mom or Dad for taking away the iPad. His immature thinking makes him imagine that inanimate things have similar feelings to him so he may think, "Anything that loud must be really angry and must want to hurt me."

Though it seems counterintuitive, when Jack compulsively asks to watch a scary movie over and over, it may be because he is trying to overcome or master his fear of the shark and its big, frightening teeth. Unfortunately, that only makes the problem worse. It would be much better if his parents would step in and turn off the scary images, then reassure Jack that they know how frightening and confusing such things can be.

Stress of any kind can also make children anxious and fearful. As wonderful as moving to a new house may be, it means the loss of a child's familiar, known world. All change is hard for little kids, so parents do well to stay closely attuned to their child's reactions during times of transition. In order to minimize her overwhelming feelings, it helps to carefully prepare her for what's coming.

Never scoff at or dismiss your child's fears, or try to jolly him out of them, no matter how unreasonable they seem to you; they are very real to him. Resist the temptation to say that big boys don't cry or tell him to buck up and be a man. Instead, try to empathize with his feelings. Comfort him and let him know that even if he gets angry and screams at you, you still love him and know that, after all the screaming is over, he really loves you, too, and that his good, loving feelings will come back.

Don't say you will chase that monster to make it go away; that will just reinforce your child's fear that there really is a monster under the bed. Try to discover exactly what this irrational fear is about, asking things like, "What do you think the monster will do?" This may help you learn what is worrying him and allow you to talk it through calmly, assuring him that you are the parent and it's your job to keep him safe.

And be sure not to sneak out of the house without saying goodbye to your child; that only reinforces his worry that you might go away and never come back. Be sure to let him know when you are leaving, telling him far enough ahead of time so that he can prepare—but not so far ahead that he spends a lot of time worrying about it. Of course, there may be tears and, if there are, don't try to jolly him out of them by telling him how much fun he'll have with the sitter. Acknowledge his unhappy feelings and assure him that you will return—and that you'll miss him, too.

As your child grows, provide firm limits appropriate to his or her age. It's up to parents to provide a calm and predictable schedule and surroundings as much as possible so that their child will feel safe and protected. The only way a toddler should be looking at any screens is for a very limited time and accompanied by an adult. Be mindful that the fast moving, confusing commercials that are so ubiquitous on TV can create confusion or anxiety for a child. This is why it's so important for an adult to watch with a child; that way you can protect him from such commercials whenever possible, or at least reassure him that you sometimes find them overwhelming, too.

Even TV programs and movies that are supposedly made for young children often include scary parts, such as animals with big teeth and menacing behavior. Again, we advise, it's best to approach all programs and movies cautiously (except for "Mr. Rogers" and "Sesame Street"—no problems there) and always watch along with your child so that you can reflect back what she is feeling and thus provide emotional containment and security.

Halloween and other holiday activities should be carefully screened so that very young children are not overwhelmed by scary costumes and situations. Witches, clowns, Santa Claus or anyone in costume—and especially anyone wearing a mask—can be scary to preschoolers. It really is true that they can't tell what's real and what's pretend at this young age.

As your child develops and learns more about the world, she will often feel confused and anxious. Fear is a normal part of the process of growing up. Show that you realize how big and scary the world must sometimes look to her and try to understand what the fear really is about. Give her respect, support and comfort, and have confidence in her growing ability to conquer these fears—with your help, of course.

Meanwhile, instead of letting her spend time alone with the TV or iPad—which expose her to things she can't do anything about, things that make her feel powerless, confused, and even frightened—keep the focus on things she *can* do, like helping you prepare the salad or washing the pots while you fix dinner. This will help build confidence and mastery and with it a sense of safety.

And remember: If you find that your child is especially stressed, don't hesitate to seek help from a professional who specializes in working with young children and their families.

GTR

Preschoolers' Fears

Try to remember what it was like when you were small and you lay in bed in the dark at night, afraid. If you have a better-than-average memory, you can recall the monster under the bed, the witch in the closet, the skeleton that tapped at your window with a bony finger. Maybe you smile now when you remember those fears because, of course, there was no monster, no witch, no skeleton—only shadows and a tree branch blown by the wind. You were probably 3 or 4 years old. You called for Mom or Dad to come protect you, and maybe they came and sat beside you for a while; maybe they yelled at you to go to sleep. But Mom or Dad was there, and pretty soon it was morning.

Fast forward through a year or two of mornings, to the day you realized that while they could protect you from monsters under the bed, there were real threats in the world against whom they just might be helpless. How were they going to protect you from a kidnapper climbing in the window if they were sound asleep in their bed down the hall? How were they going to save you from a fire suddenly engulfing the house? Hadn't you seen on the evening news a father crying because he'd been unable to get through the flames to rescue his little boy? What if an armed robber broke down the door? What if there was a flood, or a tornado, or an earthquake, bigger and stronger than any grown-up could possibly be? At those memories, we bet you stop smiling. That's a terrifying moment, when you realize that your parents aren't gods.

Now you're the parent, of course, wondering what to say to your fearful child when he realizes that you're not godlike. You are confident in your ability to comfort your child when he is afraid of the products of his own imagination, but you are unsure what to say when he asks about something he's seen on television or heard about from his friends, something all too real. "Is it true?" he might ask. "Did that really happen?"

You don't want to lie. But listen to the question. What is he really asking? Probably what he wants to know is, "Could that happen to me and my family?" What he needs to hear from you isn't that bad things don't happen, but reassurances that you are not helpless, that you know what to do. Yes, houses catch on fire, but you have a smoke detector, you know how to call the fire department and how to get everyone out of the house. Yes, there are tornadoes, but the house is strong. You know how to keep him safe. Those are things for *you* to worry about, not him.

Your attitude and tone of confidence will be as reassuring as the words you use. By the same token, if every time there's a flash of lightning and a clap of thunder you visibly cower and rush to switch on the weather channel, it will be noticed. Try to take control of your own fears even in a potential crisis and certainly in an actual one. Keep the TV news stories feeding our fears at a minimum. Your child doesn't need to hear the details about a recent terrorist attack around the clock. Your reaction to frightening situations is vital to your children's sense of security, so for their sake, continue to exude confidence and constancy. You can collapse later, and glue yourself to the TV if you want to, in private.

Lately we Grannies do hear a lot of questions about what to tell young children about terrorist attacks. The first thing would be the obvious and truthful: that happened far away and we don't expect it to happen here. To that we might add the wise words from Mr. Rogers: Look for the helpers. No matter what happens, there are always helpers who come to the aid of those who need them. There are many more helping people in the world than there are scary people. Those wise words may be more for you than for your children. But keeping that in mind, you will know what to say.

And then there's the Big Question that they are going to ask sooner or later: Are *you* going to die? A Victorian parent might have answered, "Yes, I am going to die and you are going to die; everyone is going to die, so you'd better be very, very good every day because it could be your last." Those Victorian parents must not have realized what the children were really asking: "Are you going to die when I am still little and so desperately in need of you?" Your answer should be more like this: "I'm not going to die for a very long time, and I'll be here to take care of you until you are grown up and have children of your own."

Pardon us for a diverting story about one of the Grandmothers' adorable grandchildren. One very precocious 3-year-old girl asked her grandma when she was going to die. Grandma took her on her knee and gave her several paragraphs about the seasons of life, and how she planned to be around until the child had children of her own, until her mommy was a grandmother, and that all this was very beautiful and not at all sad. The little girl listened quietly, and then asked, "When you die, can I have your shoes?"

So we are advised to listen carefully to our children's questions, and also to what they say when they don't know what questions to ask, or if they don't seem satisfied with our reassurances. Ask, "Why do you think it could happen?" Or, "You look worried; I'm wondering what worries you." Try to find out what he or she has been told or observed or imagined, and don't dismiss those fears, not even the monster-under-the-bed ones. Take his worries seriously, but also assure him that you know how to keep him safe.

KSB

Childhood Frustrations

No amount of parenting can prevent or erase frustrations from our children's lives, nor should it. Difficult experiences will always be a part of life, and we parents should allow the opportunity for them and give children our support through those trying times. It's through trial and error that we all learn.

The youngest member of a family is surrounded by people who already know how to do so many things. These children see the ease with which others dress themselves, tie their shoes, ride a bike, etc., and do not realize that practice was necessary to master these skills. When a child watches his older brother, he thinks that all you have to do to ride a two-wheeler without training wheels is put your hands on the handlebars, push the pedals with your feet and off you go!

When their first attempts do not bring good results, children often feel little, angry and overwhelmed with the activity. They may cry with frustration, throw a tantrum and stomp off, saying, "It's too hard. I don't want to do it anyway!" Mom and

Dad often become frustrated, too, and are tempted to "do for" their child.

But those who can "feel with" the child will be able to reassure her that she is fine just the way she is and that needing help is OK. We are there to give her a hand. Breaking down the process into small, manageable steps helps. Letting the child do what she can by herself and helping her with things she can't will reinforce her "growing up" side.

Mom or Dad can say, "I'll hold your sock open for you so you can push your toes in. Now, can you push your whole foot in? Good, now pull up the back and your right foot is done!" The same procedure can be adapted for each article of clothing. Soon your child will be putting on most of them by herself.

They can help her learn to ride a two-wheeler by directing her: "Push your foot down on the top pedal and then the other pedal is ready to push down with your other foot. Look ahead to where you're going and steer the handlebars just the way you do on your trike. I'll be holding on to the back of your bike so you won't fall."

She will have to struggle with some tasks more than others. Assure her that most kids can't do some things right away; that they need to keep trying. All too often and with good reason it's tempting to take over to get the job done, especially if time is a factor or it is frustrating for us to watch her struggle. Have you ever had to restrain yourself from giving her the next piece for a puzzle or shape box, or from putting your hands over hers to show her the "right" way to use scissors? Your child needs to feel the pleasure of trying, working hard, then succeeding through her own efforts.

Another important role for Mom or Dad, besides being the teacher, is being the "admirer." Even though his first attempts may be clumsy, his smallest efforts should be appreciated. "You really tried hard that time. I'm glad you're not giving up. C'mon, let's practice some more." We can begin to see how sincere admiration of his hard work and stick-to-it-ness energizes him and keeps him at it.

It takes a lot of patience to be our child's partner through all the trials and frustrations when he is learning something new, but it will be more than worth it when we hear his triumphant, "Look, I can do it by myself!"

GS

Birthday Celebrations

The candles are lit and everyone is singing: "Happy birthday, dear Ethan, happy birthday to you." But Ethan is definitely not a happy birthday boy. Tears are rolling down his cheeks, and the wish he's making as he blows out the candles is for everyone to just go away and let him play with that cool-looking truck he's eyeing in the pile of newly opened presents.

How can this be? This was supposed to be a perfect celebration for Ethan's third birthday, held at a special party venue you booked for the occasion. All 15 kids from Ethan's preschool class plus his five cousins were invited. There was a magician to entertain them, pizza, a special rocket ship cake that you slaved over, and a piñata to whack away at. What more could a child want? Well, maybe pony rides—but that's for next year.

In our competitive society, many parents view their young children's birthday parties as epic events requiring them to keep up with—or even outdo—other parents. It's easy to get swept up by the peer pressure, to think, "Madison's party was so lovely; the girls and their mothers went to a fancy hotel for lunch, then to the ballet to see "The Nutcracker." What can we do to compare with that?"

We Grandmothers have heard this situation referred to as the "Birthday Party Arms Race" and we agree with that description. In an attempt to give their child the very best, parents end up spending outlandish amounts of money and going crazy with elaborate planning. In the process, they lose sight of what would make the occasion truly enjoyable for their child. At best, the expense of money and energy is unnecessary. At worst, it can set the stage for a major meltdown. A young child is easily overwhelmed—by too many people, too much going on, and even, believe it or not, too many presents. Despite the fabulous accounts you may read on some mommy blogs, or the tantalizing images you may see on Pinterest, less is usually more when it comes to celebrations for young children.

Parents' tendency to overreach in planning birthday parties is understandable. Mom and Dad may feel guilty that, what with all the demands and distractions of work and family life, they are not giving their kids the time and attention they think they should. So they try to make it up to them by throwing a grand and glorious birthday party. The lure of convenience may add to the escalation, with parents thinking that by holding the party at some special venue like the Little Gym they can avoid spending the rest of the weekend cleaning the house.

But try to look at the situation from Ethan's perspective. How old is he? A good rule of thumb is to invite the same number of kids as the age of the child, so three guests would be perfect for Ethan's third birthday. Send a treat to the preschool so he can celebrate with his classmates there; let the actual party be a smaller, more intimate affair. Also limit the event to a manageable length of time. Two hours is plenty for a preschooler, so be sure to state the hours on the invitation so everyone knows what to expect.

Limiting the number of guests also solves the problem of too many gifts, which many parents complain about these days, and the solutions that we grandparents are appalled to see. We have heard of parties where gifts were collected from arriving guests and put into a big garbage bag to be opened by the birthday child later. Apparently the hosts assumed that the kids were likely so greedy that they would get upset when they saw all those lovely gifts and want them for themselves, so best to put them out of sight until everyone has gone home. Then there's the distressing situation of young guests not even knowing what's inside the pretty packages they have brought because Mom picked out the gifts online, ordered them gift-wrapped, and handed them over to her kid to deliver to the birthday child just as she dropped him off at the front door.

Preschoolers are just learning about parties. Being a guest involves thinking about the birthday girl, selecting a gift they think she will like and then having the pleasure of watching her open it and receiving her thanks for their thoughtfulness (or at least some indication that she likes it!). When there are only a few guests at the party, not only is gift giving a lovely and manageable part of the event, it is an opportunity for all the kids to experience what it means to give and receive.

Now that the gifts are opened, what shall we do? Remember that the simplest things are new and wonderful to young kids. Think of what your child loves to do. If he is a nature lover, go to a nearby park and have a simple scavenger hunt for acorns, bird feathers and, yes, even a piece of litter (can't start too early with cleaning up the environment—just don't forget to bring plenty of hand wipes). If it's a nice day, spread a cloth on a picnic table and let the kids ice and decorate some cupcakes, play a few games, and go home.

If your daughter would love a tea party, invite the guests to bring their dolls. The girls could make the sandwiches—and cut them to tea party size—and, of course, pour the pretend tea for themselves and their dolls. A fun craft activity, perhaps dried flowers mounted on cardboard with a popsicle-stick frame, would be a nice favor for guests to take home.

The planning and preparation can be as meaningful and fun for the birthday boy or girl as the party itself, so involve your child as much as possible. Picking out the invitations and decorations at the store or making them yourselves, icing the cake, setting the table and filling the goody bags are all major ingredients of a memorable occasion for your son or daughter.

When you plan a child-focused birthday party, you will have a much happier child. And by staying within a budget and avoiding a massive cleanup, you will also be a happier parent. Once you resist getting caught up in the birthday party arms race, you will be surprised at how rewarding such a simple occasion can be. Save the elaborate party for the bar mitzvah, quinceanera or wedding reception. By then your child will be old enough to take the extra attention and excitement in stride and appreciate each occasion for what it represents—a memorable milestone in his life.

GTR

Halloween

Dear Grandmothers,

Last year, my 3-year-old helped me hand out treats on Halloween. We were having a lot of fun until a child dressed as a witch came to the door. Amelia was terrified—she ran and hid under a table and wouldn't go near the door the rest of the evening. What can I do to make Halloween less traumatic for her this year?

In our response to Amelia's mom, we congratulated her for taking her child's fears seriously and having the foresight to think (well in advance of October 31) about how to avoid having them stirred up again. Halloween hype seems to start earlier every year—the minute the back-to-school sales are over, stores put out their displays of skeletons, witches and monster masks. Parents may be taken by surprise when their young children start getting overexcited or nervous, even misbehaving in advance of the occasion. They may not realize that such behavior is all about the upcoming season of scare.

We suspect that the reason parents are surprised that their preschool kids are overwhelmed and unhappy is that they are remembering how much they loved this holiday when they were young. And once they become adults, they anticipate the day when they have kids of their own and can take part in it again. In their eagerness to re-experience all the excitement, many parents aren't aware of their preschoolers' developmental stage and expose them to things that may be too much.

We want to issue an important caveat: When you remember all the fun you had trick-or-treating with your friends, watching a scary movie or visiting a haunted house, it is certainly not your preschool years you are remembering but elementary school. Many parents remember only those school-age Halloweens and think that those activities are what it's all about, even for the littlest kids. But they're not. Big kids like to be scared and grossed-out; their brains and nervous systems have matured to the point where they thrive on the thrills and chills. But that stuff is just too much for preschoolers.

Most importantly, little kids have not reached the stage where they can distinguish what is real from what is pretend. As a result, they believe everything they see. In the case of the 3-year-old mentioned above, Amelia may have thought that the villain of the fairy tale "Hansel and Gretel" had shown up at her door, intent on doing serious harm to any little girls she could find. No wonder she ran and hid. Wouldn't you?

Though you may talk to your preschooler about the difference between what's pretend and what's real, she just doesn't understand this distinction. Despite her brave assertion that "I know it's not real," she may still be confused and frightened when confronted by witches, skeletons, ghosts and monsters—

anyone wearing a mask. And it's not just the trick-or-treaters that can cause alarm. All the scary props of the season—the cobwebs and spiders, the flying bats and haunted graveyards—can also be frightening and confusing to a very young child.

So, what can you do to help your preschooler as Halloween season comes around? Protect her from spooky TV shows (even many commercials are overwhelming and frightening or, at the very least, confusing). Try to avoid taking her along when you need to go into stores where gruesome monster masks and eerie decorations are on display. Or, if you find yourselves in such a place, leave as quickly as you can. Be sure to let your child know you understand her fears and that you may even get spooked sometimes at Halloween yourself.

Be on the lookout for signs that your child is overwhelmed, overexcited, scared. Is she running around excitedly, or does she cling to you, have her fingers in her mouth? Any unusual behavior, at home or at preschool or child care, at this time of year should make you wonder if she's confused or frightened. This should prompt you to ask her if she is worried about something. Then you can listen carefully to her answers and try to tease out any concerns she may be expressing.

Just your recognition of her nervousness will reassure her and help her to calm down. If she can tell you what she is worried about, don't try to talk her out of her fears; acknowledge them and try to figure out a way to help her manage. Knowing that you understand and will help to protect her is just what she needs in this situation.

It's also good to let your child decide how much she wants to participate in Halloween activities and to respect her wishes. Give her a calmed-down, low-key Halloween: a costume, no mask; trick-or-treating at a few friends' or neighbors' houses well within her familiar comfort zone. Forgo the witches and ghosts for now; pumpkins and cute black cats can make for delightful, nonthreatening decorations.

So have fun this year, but be on the lookout for things that are "too much." All too soon your child will be ten and begging you to help her turn the garage into a haunted house.

GTR

Talking to Kids about Disabilities

We've become accustomed to seeing people with disabilities in schools, theaters and grocery stores and so may not be prepared for the time our very curious 4-year-old sees a man with cerebral palsy and blurts out, "What's the matter with him?" What do we do or say at that moment?

We know the question has been overheard, and we are embarrassed. We certainly don't want to hurt the man's feelings, and our mind races over a thousand answers. We often settle for silencing more questions and escaping into the next aisle, or telling her that asking questions like that hurts the man's feelings.

During the preschool years, children's bodies are changing rapidly and they're learning what they can and cannot do. It's also a time when children believe that almost everything that happens is because of something they've said or done or even thought. This can cause children to worry when they see someone whose body is different. The little girl asking about the man with cerebral palsy might think he did something wrong to cause him to look that way, or that she might catch what he has.

When Mom urgently whispers in reply, "Shh! It's not nice to ask," this little girl's anxiety doubles. Mommy's message suggests that it's not safe to talk about it, and the girl's questions are silenced.

We often forget that our preschoolers are keen observers; they take cues from our behaviors and our words, or lack of them. We would never want to give our children the impression that someone with a disability is to be feared and avoided. We also need children to begin to understand that the disability does not mean that person is without feelings, intelligence, humor and family. But many of us have not had significant experiences with people with disabilities and really don't know what to say. Our curious 4-year-old needs assurance that it's all right to ask questions. And when she does, she needs simple, clear answers.

Nothing our little girl says will be new to the person living with cerebral palsy or to someone with a large facial birthmark or other noticeable difference. We can try to predict the questions before they arise. In a calm voice we might say, "I notice you are looking very hard at the woman with the large mark on her face. You look worried. It's called a birthmark. Sometimes people are born that way. It is not anything you can catch. We can talk about it in the car, on the way home, if you have more questions."

Often we won't know why someone uses a wheelchair or speaks differently, and if we haven't anticipated the loud questions, a simple answer can be provided. "I don't know exactly why he is in a wheelchair, but I know wheelchairs are the way people can get around when they have trouble walking or can't walk at all." If you're comfortable doing so, you could engage the person with the disability: "My little girl is curious about your wheelchair." You might also offer to get something off the top shelf for him.

The important thing is our own attitude and awareness of the message we convey. We often shrink from thinking beyond feeling sorry for the mother pushing a developmentally delayed 5-year-old in a stroller, and our own unease results in our busying ourselves with shopping or pointing out the colors on the cereal box. We don't want to hurt people's feelings; letting our child know this and that her questions can be answered later is very important. We don't know the reasons why that woman is "very fat" or looks very "old" or is "bent over", but it is not something we want to discuss within her hearing. "Some people have a hard time when they are very fat. I think it hurts their feelings to overhear people talk about them and not directly to them. We don't want to do that. You can always ask me your questions later." Our answers will better convey the right message if we educate ourselves about different disabilities. We can learn more about ways that changing attitudes and modern technology are helping to integrate everyone into our society and share that information with our children.

Knowing when to answer the child's question within hearing of the person with the disability and when to briefly defer it is a hard call. We will be able to determine this better when we become aware of both our and our child's understandings and reactions. Everyone understands things differently; we do, our children do, and so do people with disabilities.

MLK

Moving

The big people in the family decide (or are forced to accept) that they need a new nest—a larger one, or a more affordable one, maybe, or one in a better school district. They find the perfect place and show it, with great fanfare, to their preschooler. The preschooler, when he finally catches on to what this crazy plan is all about, bursts into tears.

Moving from one home to another, whether halfway around the world or merely to another part of town, is upsetting, literally as well as emotionally. Everything must be packed, moved, changed. Young children's sense of security depends in large part on familiar surroundings and schedules, on predictability. They cannot be expected to understand why their parents might think a move is such a great idea. For them, a move can be devastating.

So before we start ordering a U-Haul and measuring the room sizes to see if the old rugs will fit, let's talk about feelings.

First, yours: By day you may be excited and may enjoy telling friends about the charms and advantages of your new place. Or, if it's a move you don't want to make, you may be angry and frustrated. But either way, in the middle of the night, you wake up overwhelmed by all the work you're going to have to do to get your family safely settled again. You worry about finding the time to plaster and paint; you fret about finances; you grow wistful remembering bringing a small infant home from the hospital to this very room. You are anxious, unsettled and at least a little sad.

What you feel in the middle of the night is what your child is feeling around the clock. Of course, he often goes off to play or watch television, appearing to have forgotten about the whole thing. But when he hears you talking about the move or watches you hauling in the boxes and emptying the bookcase, he grows anxious, unsettled and more than a little sad. Intuitive little sponge that he is, he picks up on your anxiety.

To the degree that it is possible, let him make some small choices since he couldn't make that big one. Let him decide where his toys will go, the placement of his bed, where you will plug in the nightlight in his new home. Let him help with the move itself, including the packing. Help him keep track of his belongings, making them the last things to go in the van—or better yet, let them ride with him in the family car.

Make pictures or a little book using stick figures to represent your child, Mom, Dad and dog Spot. Draw the moving van and the car taking them from the old house to the new one. You can fill in the words with your child watching, listening and adding ideas. Or get a children's book about moving from the library and read it together several times. Young children have difficulty understanding time, so a paper chain, with each link representing a day until moving day, might also be helpful. Every day remove a link so that he has a concrete image of the time passing and can begin to picture how long it's going to be until the moving van comes.

Because you're anxious yourself about this move, probably the last thing you want to hear about is your child's anxiety. His sad and even angry feelings just make you feel guilty. You are tempted to do all you can to jolly him out of his unhappiness or change the subject when he asks questions like, "Why can't we stay right where we are?"

But all the same, here are some of the things you might say: "Of course you're sad to be leaving the place where we live now. Of course you're going to miss Mrs. Lockland across the hall and the cookies she gives you. Of course you're going to miss your playground and the bedroom ceiling that we put glow-in-the-dark stars on and the window where you could wave to the garbage men. Mrs. Lockland and your playground friends and the garbage men are going to miss you, too."

What not to say: "You're going to love our new place much more than the old one! Did you see how big your and your brother's new bedroom is? We're right down the street from a beautiful park, and I think there's a girl your age right next door, and how about those curtains that we saw at Target with the whole solar system on them? Much better than stars on the ceiling!"

Let him be sad. Or mad! Hold him in your lap, tell him you understand and let him cry or rage. Don't tell him how he ought to feel or try to cheer him up. Give him time. His real security is you, not the house or apartment he lives in, and soon he will be loving this new one because you and the passing days have made it home.

KSB

The New Baby

"I really wanted a kitty, but they brought home a baby sister. She is very little and mostly sleeps and eats. Sometimes when I lean over her bassinet, she looks at me for a long time, and when I pat her hand, she grabs my finger and holds on tight. I like that because I think she likes me. When she cries, Mommy picks her up and rocks her. When I tried to climb up on Mommy's lap, too, Daddy said, 'You're a big 3-year-old girl, you can sit in your own chair.' I stuck my thumb in my mouth. Once I tried to lie down in the baby's tiny bed while Mommy was giving her a bath, but it made my legs hurt. Mommy told me to quit being silly and please get her another towel. I like it when Mommy says I'm her big helper, but sometimes I don't want to be a big girl.

"One day when Grandma was visiting, Mommy put the baby in her stroller and we went to the park. Mommy said I could push the stroller, but when I pushed it a little too fast, Mommy said I was being unsafe. My baby sister liked it, though, and started to cry when I stopped. Grandma found a nice bench near the water so we could feed the ducks. While I was feeding the ducks, some ladies walked past the bench and stopped to look at my baby sister in her stroller. They made all kinds of baby noises, smiled at her and patted her hand. When I ran up to tell them about all of the ducks I had fed, they didn't even look at me. Grandma said, 'Shh! You'll scare your baby sister with that loud voice!' I kicked the stroller and grabbed her bottle. When I started to drink from it, Mommy took it away and gave me a juice box. I told her *I* was the baby."

Being toppled from the "Queen" or "King" pedestal when a baby brother or sister joins the household can be very hard on a 3-year-old who has until recently been the only one needing attention and care. At the same time, though, the 3-year-old has had growing-up urges and likes being able to "do it myself!" It helps to understand and talk with her about both of these tugs within her and help her balance them. If this can be a gentle transition, she will be better able to enjoy accomplishing growing-up tasks and like becoming a bigger girl.

A child has no specific memories of those pre-verbal infant days, so she cannot remember that she was once a baby who was cared for, admired and played with just as her baby sister is now. But she does have "feeling memories" of those warm, pleasurable times when she was fed, bathed, rocked, patted and sung to. Those feelings of closeness can be recalled by describing how Mommy, Daddy, Grandma and Grandpa used to love doing these same things with her when she was an infant. Sharing "when you were a baby" stories is the perfect time to get out the albums of pictures you took then. Don't be surprised when she wants to hear about and see them over and over again! She might enjoy the thought of starting her own new album with pictures of the growing-up things she can do now. It might help her to enjoy her new role as big sister more by asking her to help with making an album of her little sister's pictures to show her when she gets older.

Children ages 4 through 6 may have some of these feelings, but they're usually not as prominent. The older child is farther away from the needs of infancy and more independent. Her world and interests have widened, leaving her less in need of her parents' exclusive attention. If parents do not ask too much of her before she is ready, the older child may enjoy being Mom's go-and-fetch helper with the baby or playing "Peek-a-boo" or "Patty Cake" to entertain her for a short time. She will like the feeling of teaching her something and having her little sister's attention.

The 2-year-old and younger child whose life is intruded upon by a new brother or sister cannot be expected to be the big sister when she is still a baby herself. The toddler probably still needs her parents' help in caring for bodily needs. She is not her own person yet and is still dependent on a parent's or caregiver's presence to venture on to new things. Watching the baby nursing or drinking from a bottle will be very difficult for her, especially if she is being weaned. Help her feel proud that she can drink from a cup just like the big people do. Toilet training may have to be put on hold for a while until she prefers being clean instead of "going in her pants" like a baby. Patience and praise are key for parents when trying to help their firstborn move on.

Parents always have the hope that their offspring will love one another from the beginning, but this is usually a mixed bag for the older siblings. They are asked to "kiss your baby sister," "pat her gently," "don't bump the stroller," etc. They can enjoy this closeness but can also become carried away with their simultaneous feelings of affection and resentment. At times, they may be aggressive and hurtful to the baby. Resentment is a normal feeling, and parents can help the child by acknowledging those feelings: "One part of you is loving her and another part is making you do mad things. But I can't let you hurt the baby. Are you mad because you feel left out? Why don't you sit with me and look at a book while I'm holding the baby? We can look at it together if you turn the pages."

It helps to acknowledge that a child's anger at a baby sister is fueled by her anger at Mommy for not being as available as she was before the baby came. "It makes you so mad that I'm busy with the baby. I still love you very much, and I'm watching all the time while you are doing so many things for yourself." Identifying a child's anger can open up a pathway for your child to experience the loving feelings toward the baby sister. These loving feelings are more authentic than the ones parents try to force on their children ("But you love your little sister, give her a big kiss!"). And, in time, as the baby is more responsive to the attention of her big sister, they can begin to form that unique sibling relationship that can become so special as they grow up together.

GS

When You Need a Sitter

There are times when parents must leave their child in the care of others overnight or longer to tend to out-of-town family matters or attend a function where children are not invited. When this need arises for the first time, they might have some concerns, especially if their child already fusses when a sitter comes for just the evening.

If the sitter can be someone your child already knows, such as a member of the extended family or a good friend, so much the better. There is already a relationship forming, and the sitter knows some of the family routines and where to find things. However, if none of these options is available, you may have to choose a sitter your child has never met but has good references and is recommended by someone whose judgment you trust. As parents, you will want to meet and interview her before she comes to your house to meet your child. Not too far ahead of the time you leave, you will want to tell your child of your upcoming plans and who will be staying with him/her while you're away.

Your child will probably protest and won't understand why she cannot go with you. She will feel angry and left out. The best way to get over these feelings is to have your child be a part of the planning. For example:

- She can help you pick out the clothing she will wear while you're gone and put it in a special place.
- She can be a part of planning the menus for the meals she and the sitter will have together.
- You can let her pick out the games she might like to play with the sitter.
- You could take her to the library to choose some new books they can read together.
- She could help plan an outing while Mom and Dad are gone—the park/playground, the zoo, going to the library for story time.

As for you parents: Even though there may be protesting that makes you feel guilty about leaving your unhappy child, don't be tempted to try to sugarcoat the feeling by telling her about all the fun things she'll be doing with the sitter while you're gone. Instead sympathize with her and tell her that you'll do the following to help take the sting out of her missing feelings:

- Show her on the calendar the day you are leaving and mark it. Then mark the day you'll be coming home. She can see how short the time will be.
- Leave a couple of short notes with the sitter that she can read to her while you're gone.
- Make a plan for a telephone or video chat session each day you're gone to reassure her that you're thinking of her.

- Suggest to the sitter that she ask your child to draw some new pictures for the refrigerator to show and surprise Mom and Dad when they come home.
- Leave a picture of the family together for her to look at so that she will have a tangible connection when she feels she's missing you the most. Tell her you'll be missing her, too.

When the leaving day arrives, you hope you've thought of everything—notes for the sitter, the name, number and address of where you'll be. The bags are packed and in the car. The sitter has come and already has your little girl engaged in the game or book you suggested. You are tempted to sneak out without saying "goodbye" and risking an upset. Don't you dare! When your child finds that you have gone without a hug or goodbye, she will really feel abandoned. It's much better to go to her, tell her you are leaving, and give her your hugs. Tell her you will call her when you get to where you're staying, and now she and the sitter can finish the story or game they had started. Maybe there will be tears, but you know that you and she will live through them.

Let me tell you a true story that one of our Grannies told about when she stayed with her 4-and-a-half-year-old grand-daughter while her parents were on a trip. She relates, "It was bedtime. They had called, and after they hung up, she was crying on her bed. The grandmother said, 'Oh, Jadey, I know how hard it is to have Mommy and Daddy away. Would you like me to read to you before you go to sleep?' She raised herself up on her elbows and cried out, 'NO—I just want to lie here and miss my mommy and daddy!' and she again flopped down on her tummy." Her granny reminds us that "We ALL want to do that at different times in our lives—well beyond 4 or 5 years of age!"

So, you did it! You spent a weekend away and feel refreshed

even though the planning felt endless. Don't be surprised if the first hugs and kisses you get when you return home are followed by your child ignoring you. She might even find a reason to become angry with you about something. Maybe the gift you brought her was "dumb." Maybe what you're preparing for dinner smells "yucky." She might fuss about going to bed because "it's not fair" that you get to stay up later.

This reaction is pretty normal for a young child who has had to "suck it up" and stay with a sitter over night for the first time. She felt left out then; now it's your turn. All of the careful planning and good preparation in the world can't make up for the fact that you left her behind and had managed without her. But, manage you did—and so did she! Point this out to her and how pleased you all can be to have accomplished such an important milestone.

GS

Scary Church Stories

Dear Grandmothers,

One of the kids at my son's preschool told him about the cru-cifixion and what happened with all the exact details, and he was horrified. Telling him about Easter Sunday did not make him feel better. He has been crying about this at night and is afraid of regular pictures of Jesus in a book. I hope it's okay to ask this question because it's about religion and everybody has their own opinion. I just wanted to know if any of you grand-mas ever ran into a situation like this and what you did.

Thank you.

—Worried Mother

Dear Worried Mother,

You know what they say about avoiding the topics of politics and religion. But that rule doesn't apply to the Grandmothers. We are glad to try to answer your difficult but excellent question.

We have two side observations on the subject of friends who tell our children frightening things: One, the friends are scared themselves, and try to relieve their fear by scaring someone else; and two, it can be very difficult to protect our children from terrifying stories. Even if our children don't see the scary movie/ television program/book themselves, one of their friends is sure to tell them about it.

But what to do about your child who is having nightmares about Jesus? Already you have done the most important thing: You took your child seriously; you didn't try to make him feel better with platitudes; you listened, you empathized. You didn't burden him with theological concepts that he wouldn't understand and that would trouble him further. Crucifixion is indeed a hideously cruel fate to contemplate.

We adults who have been looking at paintings, carvings and other reproductions of the crucifixion all our lives have become somewhat accustomed to the idea, not allowing ourselves to think about the cruelty in detail. But a sensitive child learning about it for the first time might understandably be horrified. You have probably already told him that the picture of Jesus on the cross is hard for all of us to look at and think about, and that you are not surprised that the story makes him scared and sad.

First you listen, realizing that preschool children think ego-centrically, hearing things in the context of "if it happened once, then it could happen to me or my family." Perhaps he will have trouble articulating his fear, and you will have to listen carefully to hear his very concrete interpretation of what his friend told him. You might ask him what he thinks might happen because of this story. Then, when you are sure you have heard him and that he feels understood, you might try comforting and reassuring him with whichever of the following seem most applicable, or a combination:

• Jesus lived far, far away and a long, long time ago. What

happened to him won't happen now to you or anybody you know. We will keep you safe at home, and your teachers and the people who are in charge of our city will keep our neighborhood safe.

• The picture of Jesus on the cross can be very scary, and you don't need to look at it or be worried by it. When you are older you may be ready to understand more about Jesus; then the worry won't feel so big.

• Jesus was a man who wanted to help people talk to one another, to use words instead of hurting. Unfortunately, there were some bad guys who hadn't gotten help to use words, and they were mean to him. That was long ago before people had TV and cars and a lot of the safety rules we have now. Now, people work very hard to help each other to use words. They can even help bad guys learn to use words.

You didn't mention if church attendance has become a problem, but we can certainly imagine it becoming one. Children can be introduced to religion gradually, starting simply with messages about how to be kind and loving to our family and friends. If it is a family tradition to go to church and the figure of Jesus on the cross is unavoidable, do lots of planning with your child ahead of time. Perhaps the child can bring a coloring book and focus on that during the service, or perhaps the adults can take turns staying outside with the child. It wouldn't be helpful to contaminate his introduction to religion by forcing situations that frighten him.

With that kind of loving attention and acceptance of his fear as very real, the fear will slowly fade.

KSB

PART THREE

Feelings Speak Louder than Words

Building Emotional Resilience

Believe it or not, your children watch you, antennae up and vibrating, your every waking hour. They know if you are angry or worried, even if you speak in a controlled, well-modulated tone. So be honest with them, admitting your frustrations. They will learn from you not only to express their own feelings but the words to use. And you don't want to try to talk them out of their true feelings, either.

Listen.

Excitement vs. Fun

In most circles, "exciting" and "excitement" are positive words often considered synonymous with "fun." A movie, a television program, even an activity for young children is praised for being exciting. Using the common definition, the opposite of "exciting" is "boring," and "boring" is to be avoided at all costs.

We fear, in fact, that some of you think you are not being the exemplary parents that you strive to be if your child isn't being given exciting things to do the livelong day. If he tells you he's bored, you think you've failed him, and you scurry around trying to pick up the pace. Please reconsider.

The term "excitement" can also refer to agitation, overstimulation and loss of control—the opposite of "calm." Parents, observing their over-excited children running around in circles, coming close to knocking over the birthday cake, Christmas tree or each other, may exhort them to stop and "calm down." These moments are definitely NOT "fun"—especially when a child, in addition to the cake or the tree, suffers some damage.

The term "fun" as well can be used to refer to activities that are not necessarily "exciting." Reading a book, even a quiet one like *Goodnight Moon*, for example, can be fun but not exciting. Reading one of those books with all the built-in computerized quacks and sirens, in contrast, can be exciting but not much fun after the novelty has worn off.

We find that clarification of the difference between fun and excitement can help us assess which activities are and aren't helpful to our children in the process of growing up; which activities bring pleasure and mastery; and which activities lead to distress and loss of control. This clarification seems particularly helpful to address during times of celebration, holidays and birthdays, when the media and family customs tend to promote "excitement" as if it were "fun," when it isn't always.

Is it really fun to be bombarded with advertisements and floor-to-ceiling rows of toys, the majority of which you are told you can't have? Is it really fun to have your home invaded by dozens of children you don't know very well who want to play with your most precious belongings and eat up all that beautiful cake, including the part with your name on it, and then smash with a stick that lovely piñata your mom bought for you only yesterday? Is it really fun to put on a costume with a mask you can't see out of and walk up and down the streets with terrifying-looking creatures, who shove you out of the way if you can't say "trick or treat" fast enough? Is it really fun to be at a party with forty other adults and children where so many things are going on that you can't make sense of anything and you end up racing some other child up and down the stairs over and over until you slip, fall down, and end up with a bleeding lip? And what if in the midst of one of these "fun" activities you lose control in your over-excitement, hit somebody, and get yelled at? How much fun is that?

"Excitement" is a physical/emotional state that occurs in response to stimulation. Some call "excitement" an impulse. It can be pleasurable when the degree of stimulation is manageable. It stops being "fun" when the impulse stimulated becomes bigger than a person can manage; that is, when the excited impulse takes over and propels a person into doing something he or she wouldn't otherwise want to do.

You've already learned to spot the signs that your child is getting over-stimulated. His voice rises both in pitch and volume, his eyes narrow and his teeth clench with aggression or, if he is the victim of some other overexcited child, his eyes widen with fear and approaching tears. You feel the need to jump in and stop the running, the wrestling, the tickling before the loud laughter turns to loud sobs. You can hear your mother's words from your childhood coming out of your mouth, saying, "Now, just stop before someone gets hurt!" But you may want to squelch that impulse because you don't want to spoil the "fun." Go with your first reaction and stop the escalation of excitement before it takes over and the "fun" ends in bandages or broken table lamps or worse. Your child may even protest that he and his friends were just playing, that no one will get hurt. But he in fact is likely not enjoying this scary excitement and will quickly accept a substitute activity that you suggest.

Your child will enjoy holiday and other special celebrations the most when he feels sufficiently in control of his experiences. You can help him feel in control by providing him ways to be an active participant in as many parts of the celebration as you can: He can help make the decorations; he can set the table for the guests; he can be told ahead of time exactly what will happen and when (no surprises) and allowed to make choices where possible. You can protect him from becoming over-stimulated by pacing the activities and choosing ones appropriate to his age level.

Daily life without parties doesn't have to be exciting either. In fact, a little calm can do us all a world of good. And if when we adults are in the middle of enjoying the peace and quiet our children come to us and say they're bored, tell yourself that a little boredom is good for them. They will benefit from being challenged to come up with their own fun, using their innate imaginations and creativity.

Fun doesn't have to be exciting. In fact, it usually isn't.

KSB

Painful Feelings

Of all the developmental tasks that we hope our growing child will successfully master, none is more demanding on the parent—who is also growing—than the child's learning to express his feelings. We want him to tell us when he is angry or sad or frustrated or annoyed. We are hopeful that if he acquires a complete feelings vocabulary, he will be able to cope with these emotions. We want this so much that we even have an emotions chart, illustrated with cartoon faces, posted on our refrigerator at his eye level.

We faithfully practice using these words ourselves. When our child has a temper tantrum in the grocery store, we hold our own emotions in check while we intone, "Are you feeling angry that Mommy won't buy you the cereal with the chocolate chips and marshmallows in it? But you see, Mommy is feeling worried that if you eat that kind of cereal, you won't grow up to be healthy and strong."

But then comes the inevitable day when our child breaks our

heart with her grief over her goldfish dying, or her best friend abandoning her, or her inability to stay vertical on her scooter no matter how hard she tries. We want to rush in and fix it, wipe away the tears, offer a new goldfish, a different friend, an ice cream cone, whatever it takes to make her stop telling us how sad she is. Even worse is when the grief, or fear, or both, have been caused by something we've done: leaving her all day in a child care center, perhaps, or moving the family to another house, or presenting her with a baby brother. Then we want to tell her how to feel, to move quickly to the other side of the feelings chart, to *joyful* and *proud* and *excited*. At least we want the experts to keep their promise, that if we approach potentially stressful events such as a new baby or a move with lots of talk about how the child might feel sad or angry, then the child will immediately start feeling better.

Our instinct is to protect them from all harm, from all pain. We cannot bear to watch them suffer, certainly not for a protracted period of time. So we become frustrated when all our talk about emotions doesn't seem to "work." The baby is six weeks old already, and big brother is still uncharacteristically moody. We moved a month ago, and he's still bursting into tears at nothing. Our children's painful emotions can sometimes be harder for us to endure than our own.

The developmental stage we're talking about here is, in fact, not our child's, but ours. As parents, we need to learn to tolerate the emotions that children's feelings evoke in us. We need to realize that expressing and managing feelings is not the same as eradicating them. Painful feelings will remain painful no matter what we say, no matter how we encourage our child to talk about them. They are his feelings to own and live with, and we cannot get rid of them for him, nor should we try. The point of learning to use the words on the feelings chart is not to overcome emotions but to express them more exactly and satisfyingly than he might otherwise. If he can tell us how much he misses his old house, he might not need to crayon all over the freshly painted walls in his new bedroom. If he can express his jealousy verbally, he might not pinch his baby brother when we're not looking. But he still will feel bewilderment or loneliness or discouragement or rage. It's still going to hurt.

Maybe a first step would be trying to be honest about our own feelings. When we are angry, we can say so. When we are sad ourselves about leaving the home where we have lived for the past several years, we can admit it, rather than pretend to be overjoyed with the new place. We can verbalize our feelings honestly. Our children can tell the difference between sincere expressions and stilted recitations from the feelings chart.

And as difficult as it might be for us, we can give our child time to grieve, to cry, to express his anger and disappointment, without rushing in with solutions. If we can outgrow our desire to fix everything for him and instead be so in tune with his feelings that we can help him identify them, he will have a clearer idea of what he's feeling than any cartoon face could possibly illustrate. He most needs from us what we as adults most need when we are despondent or anxious: a willing ear, some empathy, an arm around the shoulder, a hug. These gestures can make all the difference.

KSB

Kids Notice Everything

We often dismiss our young children's observational skills. Did our young daughter notice that she was the only white (or black) child on the playground? Of course not! Did our son happen to observe that all the women in the shower room were naked? Didn't seem to. How about the man without legs in the wheelchair? Well, our daughter started to stare, but we distracted her and she forgot all about it.

"Well, she didn't *say* anything."

Perhaps we are eager to believe that they don't notice physical differences such as race or handicap or gender paraphernalia because these subjects make us squirm, and we aren't sure we have the words to adequately talk about them. And of course we like to think of our children as wholly innocent and accepting, little Adams and Eves in the blissful Eden of their lives.

But all of us who have tried to walk with a young child from here to there know full well that she notices and wants to touch every bug and blade of grass and passing dog, and that the only thing she doesn't notice, in fact, is how late it is getting as she explores and investigates. So why would we possibly think she wouldn't observe something so eye-catching as breasts or skin color or legs that end at the thigh?

"So maybe she does notice."

She certainly does. Noticing is her job, and she's a lot better at it than we are. But either because she doesn't have the language at her disposal yet, or because our reaction (which she is the world's foremost expert at noticing) indicated that she is not to comment, she keeps quiet.

Meanwhile, we may be failing to notice the child's eyes growing round as silver dollars or her unusual behaviors afterward as she tries to make sense of what she's seen. For example, does the only white child on the playground start coloring her hands and face with magic markers? Does the boy you walked through the shower room begin popping in on us when we are dressing and bathing, though he never did before? And does the child who saw the man in the wheelchair start becoming hysterical at the slightest bump or skinned knee?

"So what are they thinking?"

When we don't notice and help them out, children must draw on their limited previous experience and their primitive logic in order to make sense of their observations. The conclusions they come to might not only be erroneous but frightening in their implications. (Is there something wrong with my body because it doesn't look like his/hers? Will I lose my legs, too, if I go near that man in the wheelchair?)

"How do I encourage their questions?"

Physical differences exist in our homes, of course, and we make a choice early on about whether to shield children from them. Children who start seeing family members' naked bodies at an early age will notice and may be full of questions. It's better to answer these questions ourselves, sometimes over and over again, rather than leave our children to draw their own faulty conclusions.

Sometimes we have no clues except our children's behavior to guide us, and interpretation can be difficult. But maybe our son has started gawking at us as we undress in a way that makes us feel self-conscious. Or maybe our daughter looks alarmed when she sees the man in the wheelchair and grabs tightly at our hand. We have to do our own vigilant noticing, and when we sense that one of these situations may have become overwhelming or confusing for our child, start asking our own questions. "Are you wondering about breasts, and why some people have them and some people don't?" "Are you worried about that man we saw in the wheelchair?" Gradually their questions will emerge, as you talk together about what they've seen.

Sometimes we would prefer that our children not notice. Heaven forbid that in some quiet waiting room she might ask in her high, piercing voice, "Mommy, is that man going to have a baby? Look how fat his tummy is!" When that happens we can only smile wanly, whisper to her that we'll answer her question later, and hope that the man with the paunch has a sense of humor. Later we can explain about women being the only ones who get pregnant and maybe also introduce the idea of sensitivity about other people's feelings. We will in no way scold her for her questions, however, but encourage her to ask more.

It's worth the risk. Notice what your children are noticing, because they most certainly are.

KSB

Talking to Kids about Prejudice

When up against a difficult topic like this one, we Grannies like to consult one of our favorite and most reliable sources: show tunes. We came up with three good ones for racism (and other differences among humans that seem to divide us).

"Everyone's a Little Bit Racist" (from *Avenue Q*; lyrics by Robert Lopez and Jeff Marx)

We have to admit it. We all are. But none of us wants our children to be racist, and we like to believe that if we don't bring up the subject, they will remain as innocent and bias-free as they were the day they came out of the womb. Unfortunately, they are likely to learn some biases on the subject from us, their parents and caregivers, because we will be giving ourselves away with every gesture and comment they observe from their earliest beginnings. So we must certainly behave ourselves and, even better, try to become at least a little bit less racist before we say or do something we regret. There are books we can read on the subject, discussions we can enter into, new friends we can make, if we have the courage and the true desire to raise our children to be as close to nonracist as it's possible to be.

"You've Got to Be Carefully Taught" (from *South Pacific*; lyrics by Oscar Hammerstein)

"You've got to be taught to hate and fear," the song begins. We may have been taught to hate by our parents but we certainly don't want to pass on those lessons to our children. How did our parents first start teaching us to distrust the "other"? By making a derogatory remark about a player on a football or baseball team? By pointing with disdain at people who dress differently? By telling us not to play with or to trust a new playmate for no reason that we could understand at first? By quickly crossing the street when we saw "them" coming? Or by moving out of the neighborhood? How long did it take us to catch on? Remembering how we learned to hate will help keep us from becoming purveyors of such hatred ourselves. If at all possible, give your children the opportunity to grow up with a diverse population on the street where they live, in the schools and churches they attend, in the stores and restaurants they frequent, in every fabric of their lives. That way, children will know all kinds of people as friends and neighbors, not the distrusted "other."

"Children Will Listen" (from *Into the Woods*; lyrics by Stephen Sondheim)

They certainly will. So when you hear about some injustice done in your community or beyond because of prejudice against the "other," tell your children how sad that makes you feel and how you hope that they are quick to defend a child who is maligned in that way. Bring home library books about children who look, dress or talk differently than your children do. Make multiculturalism part of your child's education, and urge your child's classroom teacher to do the same, if s/he isn't already doing so.

Fill your young children's days with the music you want them to hear.

KSB

When Your Child is Mean

Jason and Andy, both 4-year-olds, were side-by-side, building block roads and running toy cars and trucks along them. All of a sudden, Andy grabbed Jason's dump truck, pushed him over and destroyed their road. Jason looked at Andy with surprise and began to cry loudly. Andy's Mom, quite embarrassed and angry, snatched the truck from Andy and spanked him. Her reaction is understandable, but does it really help Andy to think about what he has done? Is he sorry for the way he made his friend feel, and does he want to make things better?

When a child hits, grabs, destroys others' work or says mean things, often the adult's immediate impulse is to stop him physically, make angry threats and demand explanations and apologies. When our dismay and anger leads to these kinds of reactions, we are probably not helping the child want to change his behavior. Instead of feeling remorse about what has happened, the young child feels he's the one being attacked. He feels angry that his actions have been thwarted or not understood.

If Andy had been a toddler, as yet unable to tame his impulsive behavior, a calm removal from the situation or a distraction would have probably been the best first course of action to take. Toddlers are not yet ready to feel sincerely sorry for others when they have been hurtful, but they can begin the process by witnessing the adult apologize and sympathize with the victim. Then he can relate this to the times when someone has been mean to him and how being comforted helped him feel better.

Around the age of three, even though he is still very self-centered, a child has the ability to be more in control of hurtful impulses. He begins to relate to those around him outside of his immediate family. He is more able to have regard for the feelings of other children and want to choose their companionship over indulging in hurtful impulses for his own gratification. But he needs help.

In order to feel sorry and want to make a meaningful apology, a child needs to feel bad about what he has done or caused and not like that feeling. The capacity for such is there for the very young child, but it needs to be helped and nurtured by the adults in his life. They can help him think about what kind of boy he wants to be and that only he can make that choice for himself. In order to feel sorry and take responsibility for causing a hurt, he needs a feeling of compassion. This takes knowing something of what the one he's "done unto" is feeling. It takes wanting to preserve the relationship and wishing he'd not done what he did. It takes not liking the feeling of being that person who is unkind and does hurtful things. Around ages 4 or 5, children begin to wrestle with their feelings about themselves and how they have behaved. They are struggling with their developing consciences and the increasing capacity to empathize with others' feelings. They feel better when they learn their mistakes can be corrected; then they are able to move on.

We must also remember how readily children identify with and imitate the actions of the grown-ups in their lives. If they grow up seeing their role models put down or abuse others physically or verbally, they will most likely mimic this behavior and make it a part of their own personalities.

Before being able to understand and feel these qualities of compassion, remorse, apology and wanting to make another feel better, the young child must first have experienced them for himself. He needs to have had sympathetic attention when he's been hurt or when someone has been mean to him. He needs to feel concern and protection from those around him. If he has been dealt with compassionately on these occasions, he is better able to feel for the one to whom he's been unkind.

He is able to listen to reminders such as, "Remember when Joey pushed you and took away your sand pail—how bad you felt and how mad you were? That's the way Mary feels now because you've been mean to her. I know you don't like being an unkind friend. Let's think of something we can do to make Mary feel better; then you'll like yourself better, too. I'll help you draw a picture (help you fix her block building, mend her book, etc.) to let her know you're really sorry."

When the young child cannot like the "self" he is when he is mean and hurtful—when he can "feel with" the child he's been unkind to and wishes he hadn't been—when he can participate in an apology that can help his victim feel better, he is well on his way to putting the desire for good relationships with others ahead of his self-centered impulses. He is moving toward the next step in healthy development.

GS

Understanding Bullying

Lately, we've been bombarded with stories about bullying incidents involving children, some of them resulting in tragedies. These horrific stories appall us and make us wonder what happens in a child's life that could cause him/her to want to be mean and cruel, to want to tease, belittle or even physically hurt another to this extent.

What is called "bullying" does not usually show up until a child's middle-school years, but the traits have probably been forming since early childhood. A child's actions often reflect how he or she has been treated. Early traumatic experiences such as a medical procedure or hospitalization can also make a child feel punished and alone.

When a small child is punished over and over by an adult with anger, sarcasm and/or physical hurt, he feels little and helpless, victimized. It would be hard for him to feel sorry for what he's done when given this kind of punishment let alone want to apologize or make amends. He feels he has been "done to" and wants to retaliate.

One of the things parents and caregivers need to look at

carefully is how their methods of discipline affect their child. Has he been able to show remorse for what he's done, and does he want to make things better? Or, did the hitting, yelling and threatening kind of punishment just make him angry and wanting to "get back at"? There is little relief from this kind of feeling when the child is so small and the adult so much bigger, so the fury may just lie there, fester and grow.

If a young child has continually experienced this kind of treatment, he cannot feel valued nor worth much. If he has not been helped to figure out what went wrong that caused this kind of punishment and not want to do it again, he may identify with what has been done to him in order to feel bigger. He wants to be the one who has the control so as not to have this awful feeling again.

He wants to feel the power that makes others feel weak so that he can feel big and in charge. In a misguided way, this feeling of power leads him to a false sense of being looked up to, even admired—especially when there are onlookers who stand back and do nothing.

Sometimes those who are witnessing an episode of bullying get caught up in the excitement it stimulates. They can even lose the sense of self and sensitivity that would ordinarily empathize with the child who is the bully's victim. They become a part of the "herd" that follows instead of using their better judgment. There may be elements of fear involved, too—fear that the bully may turn on them if they criticize.

It is very important that parents talk with their children about incidents like these, which they may have seen firsthand or heard about. Parents need to let children know that this kind of behavior must be stopped and that their child must let an adult know—a parent, a teacher, principal or counselor. The child cannot stop what is happening herself, but it is her responsibility to let someone know who can stop it. Assure her that this is not tattling or "ratting." It is much more serious than that.

In many of the schools where these sad incidents have happened, parents and school staff have formed groups to be aware of and look into possible situations where bullying might be going on. Ask your child's teacher what kind of procedures the school has in place if incidents of bullying are suspected. This kind of awareness should prevent a lot of mistreatment by would-be bullies and even be able to provide help for them. It can happen only if someone speaks up.

These thoughts about bullying have considered mainly the face-to-face, verbal, perhaps even physical kind. In a way these kinds of situations can be gotten at more easily than a new way that has become available only in recent years: Internet bullying. We cannot know the extent of how the Internet can be used to tease, hassle and malign others, but we know that it often happens. In fact, it has become somewhat of a game with some groups of youngsters. It is easy to do, and consciences aren't bothered as much because the victims aren't visible.

Again, parents, it's up to you—you do need to know how your child is using the Internet and what he/she is receiving and sending. Also, when kids use the more recent forms of Internet communication—texting, Facebook, Twitter and the like—the source of it is usually impossible to trace back to and detect. That's why it is so imperative that you help your child feel able to confide in you if he or she knows who the bully is. This is hard because of not wanting to "fink" and the fear of becoming the one being targeted.

In the meantime, enjoy your chilren's everyday accomplishments and let them know they are valued. When things go wrong, help them understand why, and help them figure out what you and they can do to make it better. This kind of relationship will see the whole family through the many ups and downs to come.

GS

Holiday Disappointments

"It's the most wonderful time of the year," sings Andy Williams over the PA system in Walmart, and as we pile gifts into our shopping cart, we halfway believe it. The kid riding in the cart, eyeing the decorated artificial trees and the life-sized cardboard Santas and the aisles and aisles of toys, sincerely believes it.

Her favorite TV shows, her preschool teachers, the Santa on whose lap she sat last week at the shopping mall, her older siblings and playmates—they all have convinced her of it. Everyone is as happy as happy can be during holiday time because they're all going to get exactly what they want, plus a few things they never even imagined.

And then the crash comes. Maybe it's because her divorced mom and dad didn't get back together as she had hoped. In fact, Dad didn't even show up; just left a gift under the tree. Maybe it's because she got the flu and spent most of Christmas throwing up. Maybe it's because she got in a fight with her brother over a toy they both wanted and got put in "time out" by an unusually crabby mother. Maybe she didn't get that puppy she had asked Santa to bring her. Maybe it looked like her sister got more presents than she did. Whatever the cause, if she knew the words, she would tell us that she is terribly disappointed. And if she did, *we* would be terribly disappointed.

We say we want her to tell us about her feelings; we try to teach her the words by putting a chart of their names and corresponding facial expressions on the refrigerator with magnets. We encourage her to tell us about being angry at her brother (a big improvement over smacking him, after all) or being sad that her goldfish died (she had never paid much attention to it anyway). But it's another matter altogether if that anger or sadness is directed at us. We want her to be all smiles on Christmas and to tell us that she is joyful and grateful. We definitely don't want to hear that she really wanted that Barbie doll that we thought we had talked her out of, or that she's missing the daddy we sent away without consulting her.

As parents, we need to learn to tolerate the emotions that our child's feelings evoke in us. We need to realize two things: that expressing and managing feelings is not the same thing as eradicating them; and that if we encourage our children to express their feelings, we'd better be prepared to hear things we didn't want to hear.

Painful feelings will remain painful no matter what we say, no matter how we encourage our child to talk about them. They are her feelings to own and live with, and we cannot get rid of them for her, nor should we try. Expressing them makes them no less painful, but it does make them more tolerable, especially if the child receives sincere empathy in return. The point of our child's learning to use the words on the feelings chart is not to overcome them, after all, but to be able to express them.

We don't want to sound like Scrooge, but when we're approaching the holidays, we need to prepare our children for the inevitable disappointments. One way to do this would be to ask our children what they are anticipating and then explain, if necessary, that some of their expectations just aren't likely to be met.

Of course we also might work on our own unrealistic expectations for each holiday season and be prepared not only for our children's disappointments but for our own. Then we will find it easier to listen, empathize and offer our understanding and a consoling hug before returning to the family celebration as if disappointments were a natural part of life. Because they are, even at holiday time.

KSB

Good Feelings about Giving

It was Christmas morning, and as the family sat around the little tree, under which was a modest pile of wrapped gifts, Nina could not contain herself. She ran to the tree, pulled her gifts away from the others and distributed them; one for Mommy, one for Daddy and one for Grandma. She then stood by and watched, wiggling and grinning, as they were opened.

She was almost four, and her babysitter had helped her make a card for each person by patiently spelling out "I Love You" for her to write. She decorated each one with colorful squiggles, which she encased in wrapping paper and lots of Scotch tape.

It brought to mind the time when I was seven, when I had been given a little money for Christmas shopping. I searched and searched for the perfect gift for my grandmother. I finally found it at the five-and-dime store—a large cross on a long chain. I clearly remember the feeling of not being able to wait two more days, insisting she open it early even though she was urging me to wait until Christmas morning. She loved that cross; I knew it, because she wore it on Christmas Day.

I mention these two incidents because of the differences in the ages of the children. Nina probably won't remember her excitement about giving her gifts because she was so young, but she will have good feelings about giving, which will eventually build if she's given the time and materials to create or purchase her gifts. A 7-year-old almost always remembers the minute details and the feelings that accompanied the giving.

Both these stories glow with the spirit of giving. Both speak to the making or the selection of the gift, and both illuminate the feelings that are so powerful they temporarily outweigh any thought of, "What am I getting?"

The ways in which children's gifts are received will be emotionally felt and remembered for a lifetime. Will the recipient value the gifts in genuine ways, such as displaying Nina's card on the dresser or wearing the cross?

Good feelings about giving will be discouraged if children find their special drawings thrown out with the wrapping paper or ignored and out of sight. Saying lovely things about a present and never again looking at it or referring to it suggests the praise was insincere and the thanks empty of feeling.

If they have spent special time getting their presents ready, they will be particularly sensitive to adult reactions and will track those presents. "Where is the present now?" "Is Grandma going to wear it?" "Did Uncle Vince eat any of the cookies Mommy and I made for him?"

These behaviors and good feelings about giving are the ones we love to see in our children and are eager to nurture.

MLK

First Lessons about Death

Dear Grandmothers,

My 3-year-old son Noah's hamster is looking sick and I don't know what to do if it dies. Should I run out and get another one so Noah won't know what happened? I don't want him to be sad and upset, so please help me to be prepared for this situation.
—Worried Mother

Dear Worried Mother,

This may sound odd, but you should be grateful that Noah has this opportunity to experience death in a relatively simple way, rather than with the death of a loved person. It is a chance for him to learn what death is, what is done with a dead body, and how we grieve the loss rather than ignore it.

The basic understanding of death can begin when a child is very young, when he notices dead things like insects or worms. If we use the word "dead" and explain that the bug will never move again because it is dead, we are helping him to have a concrete understanding of death in a situation that is not so emotionally charged as the death of a person he knows.

The death of a pet also provides the opportunity to show your child what is done with a dead body. He may want to hold the dead pet, even want to keep it, but we need to let him know that it will begin to smell, so we have to bury it. Putting Noah's hamster in a box with a soft cloth around it and burying it in a protected spot in the back yard, perhaps with a flower planted on the grave, allows everyone to show their feelings of sadness.

Allowing Noah time to feel sad and miss his furry companion without rushing out to buy a replacement gives him an opportunity to live with these feelings, feelings that he can bear—in fact, they are feelings he should be allowed to have, not ignored by a well-meaning parent who wants him to be happy always. Experiencing sadness and learning to live with it is one of the ways we help children build emotional muscle.

We Grandmothers certainly understand a parent's wish to spare children any distress. We also know that it's often because parents want to avoid sadness themselves. But we are doing the child a disservice if we don't allow him to experience a range of feelings and know that he can bear them.

When there is a death in the family, or in the family of a friend or classmate, Noah will at least have an idea of the answer to one of the inevitable questions: "What is dead?" And, of course, to the underlying worry of the bigger question: "Can it happen to you, Mommy and Daddy?"

You can be truthful but still reassure Noah. "No, we won't die for a long time; we're healthy, and we take care of ourselves. You'll be grown-up, and we'll be grandparents for many years." You may think you should be totally truthful and acknowledge that death is unpredictable, but to a child, because he has such a poor understanding of time, that means it could happen tomorrow or next week and can cause needless worry.

What about spiritual answers to the question of death? Noah, at 3 years old, just doesn't have the abstract thinking skills to understand God and heaven and other religious concepts. We Grandmothers prefer to help young children by looking at pictures and talking about missing the person who has died. "Everyone has a hard time understanding death. It's hard to believe that someone is never coming back, so I like to remember her and think about the things we did with her when she was alive."

However, whatever your beliefs about death, be very aware of how your child is interpreting the things he hears, and be on the lookout for any unusual behavior he may show that lets you know he is confused and worried. Imagine how scary it would be for a child to hear that Grandpa "went to sleep." How can he close his eyes at night when he imagines that death is what happens when you go to bed? Likewise, when someone says that Grammy's in heaven, he may think, "Why can't she come down from there and play with me?" Be on the lookout for signs that something is bothering your little one, and try to help him think of something that is comforting to him.

So, Worried Mother, we've told you much more about young children and their understanding of death than you were asking, but we couldn't resist this opportunity to talk about such an important issue for all parents.

Thank you for bringing it up. Good luck as you help Noah deal with the many issues of growing up and help him build the emotional muscle that he will need throughout his life—beginning with the death of a pet.

GTR

The Death of a Parent

The Grandmothers have already written about ways to help young children begin to understand death. We have suggested, when our children ask the dreaded question, "Are you going to die?" after a loved gerbil dies or when they hear about people dying on the TV, that we comfort them with "I expect to live a long time and will be right here to see you grow up."

But what do we say to help a child when a loved one close to the child, especially a parent, does die?

The death of a loved one is such a painful experience for everyone that the remaining family members sometimes fail to recognize how much even the youngest children need words of comfort and reassurance. That recognition is often overshadowed by their need to protect them and, even more, to protect themselves. Knowing they are very young, they reason that it may be better to avoid talking about the loss because they think young children probably don't fully understand what has happened or won't remember much. Also, they feel that to fall apart, to sob, to have no words and feel helpless in front of their toddler or preschooler is too overwhelming for them and for the child. Taking the needed time to help the child asks more of the remaining parent, grandparent, aunt or uncle than may be physically or emotionally possible.

But they must talk to the child! Even the youngest child is dramatically affected in so many ways. The person who cared for her and with whom she had such a strong relationship is gone. The people around her are behaving so differently, and their sadness is palpable. People are preparing food in different ways, different clothes are chosen and the familiar family routines have all suddenly changed. Family members can't even imagine ways to answer a toddler who asks unnerving questions like, "Where is Mommy? When will she come back? Who will make my cereal?"

However, these questions need to be answered as simply and concretely as possible. Possible ways to help the child might be: "Mommy was very sick for a while. She died and now she can't come back. When a person dies they can't see or hear or talk any more. It's so hard for you, hard for all of us to try to understand she won't be coming back. We are so sad, and we know you must be, too. We all loved her so much."

The surviving parent or grandparent should reassure the child that although things have changed, "Daddy and Grandma will be here with you to make sure you are safe. They will get breakfast and dinner for you and help you get your clothes ready in the morning. You may have lots of questions, so make sure to ask them."

Remember young children can understand the words you say and sense your feelings long before they can articulate the same thoughts themselves. They can also understand your words when they're right and fit with what they need to know, particularly when said by a loved and trusted adult.

The critical thing is to observe the behaviors, to try to understand what their concerns are, and above all to allow questions. Every child adapts to events differently, and each child will need to have these conversations about this loss over and over. Toddlers and preschoolers interpret death and the loss differently than they will at ages 7, 12 and 15.

Children age 5 and under are very self-centered and are likely to think everything that happens is the result of something they've said or done or thought. When children feel responsible for a death or a divorce, for example, the last thing the adults think to talk about is this aspect of a child's trying to cope with the loss. It's important to reassure children it was not their fault. It would be helpful to say, "You know it's not your fault that Mommy died. She was very sick." Just saying that could be important to the child for now and as she grows older.

Keep in mind that the most frightening questions children have may never be asked because they are terrified of hearing the answers. If the answers are filled in by the children, they are often more terrifying than the truth. The best way to help is to avoid peppering a child with questions, observe the child and listen carefully. Fears and misunderstandings may be heard or seen in new behaviors and can then be addressed.

A young child can never remember the loved one the way the adults in his life do. This parent will be remembered powerfully but in the way a 2- or 4-year-old remembers. The best gift relatives and close friends can give that child will be in stories that are told or in descriptions they are willing to write down and save. Include the most human aspects of the person who has died so the child is not left with a "perfect" person to either dismiss or try to live up to. What did Mommy do well? What did she do poorly? Did Daddy have things he loved to do or always put off doing? What made him laugh? What made her impatient? What did either parent love to do together with their children? Is there a favorite necklace, a watch that can be saved, a voice recording, samples of handwriting, or actual photographs of that parent at different ages? Can a special box full of a few of Mommy's or Daddy's keepsakes be saved for the child?

Life changes for children who have lost parents. This becomes part of their story, and they should have the words to describe this story. They are resilient and will learn to adapt to life and take in stride the many times friends refer to what their father or mother taught them or to days in school when Mother's or Father's Day gifts are being made. The world goes on and can't be expected to be aware of and adapt to each individual child's loss.

Parents, relatives and friends help so much with sharing rich memories of the parent who has died and by being part of the fabric that holds children and families together.

MLK

PART FOUR

Self Esteem Cannot Be Purchased

The Importance of Gaining Mastery

It's a very good thing that self-esteem is recognized as a desirable attribute, and that we know better than to tell our children that they are worthless and unattractive. But we should realize that its source isn't shiny trophies or monotonous recitations of "Good job!" It comes from within, through accomplishments that our children master on their own—starting with taking the first step, then toddling, then getting to the potty on time more often than not, and putting puzzles together. Moving on to exploring out of doors, running as fast as the wind, jumping into puddles, climbing up to the top of the hill, feeling like king of the world, and proud because they know they did a good job, not because we told them they did.

"Good job!" and its ilk, unless sincerely expressed, are really just a form of control. They say, "You did it *my* way, good for you!" Sugar-coated words, but controlling all the same.

Promoting Self-Esteem

"One Hundred Ways to Say 'Good Job!'" the heading on the sheet of stickers says. All one hundred, from "Awesome" to "Zero Mistakes," appear with accompanying smiley faces and abundant exclamation points. These are sold to teachers as self-esteem promoters. Teachers and children alike know them to be artificial at best, but at least they are evidence of the general awareness that self-esteem is an important commodity.

But self-esteem is not so easily promoted from without. By definition, it has to grow from within. Children who receive praise for work that they know is less than their best feel worse about themselves, not better, when they hear a perfunctory and excited "Good job!" or "Gimme a high five!" Older students feel dismissed, unworthy of a more time-consuming and honest critique of their efforts. Younger ones just feel vaguely guilty, or become mixed up with a feeling of excitement instead of pride in what they've accomplished.

It's all too easy to fall into the phony "Good job!" trap. If the admiration is sincere, the child senses that. If he distrusts the praise, however, he will feel manipulated. And if he grows to depend on the adult for confirmation that he's done a "good job," then he has not gained in self-esteem.

It occurs to us that sometimes our "Good job!" is meant more to control than to praise. We are actually saying, "Good for you; you did it *my* way; you are pleasing me." Too many "good jobs" and the kid waits only for that confirmation, doesn't bother pursuing any creative ideas of his own.

Sometimes words are unnecessary. If a child is absorbed in a project, she might well feel interrupted, even patronized, if an adult bursts in with effusive burbles and coos. It's perfectly okay to just smile and nod, and then go about one's business as the child continues with hers, permitting her satisfaction to grow within.

If words are called for, however, try something like, "You must feel good about being able to climb up to the top of that climber. You have been working hard at that. Last week you had to stop halfway up and now you're at the very top." The child will benefit from hearing what exactly is being admired, and also from reflecting on how *he* feels about his accomplishment, not how the adult feels. You certainly don't want him to start doing a "good job" only to win your praise; you want him to do a good job for the job's sake, for his own inner satisfaction.

But what if he sincerely tries, and sincerely fails? What if the climber is just too high or the shoe-tying is simply too difficult, and he comes to you wailing his discouragement? Then the admiring adult is called upon to notice the effort and intent, the tiny steps that might in time lead to an accomplishment of the difficult task, and admire those. In fact, the parent has every reason to admire persistence and patience more than the completion of a difficult task. In psychological tests, children have been observed increasing their efforts when it's their persistence that is praised rather than their success.

And then there's the matter of what you say when the first words that pop into your head aren't "Good job!" but "Terrible job!" The toys she promised to pick up are still scattered where she left them, or she gave herself a disastrous haircut with the scissors she wasn't supposed to touch. If you tell her of your displeasure, will you permanently damage her self-esteem? Of course not. In fact, the spirit of "terrible job"—although perhaps not those exact words—is the message you want to convey, as opposed to "terrible kid." If you can keep your wits about you, you might follow the format recommended for admiring her successes. Tell her exactly what she did that distressed you, and then suggest that perhaps she feels bad about what she did and will feel better if she can make amends somehow. And then help her find a way to do that. She could get to work picking up those toys or sweep up the hair that's strewn all over the bathroom floor.

Our own self-esteem is involved in whether our child can climb to the top of the climber, hop around the room on one foot, or go all day without pooping in his pants. We would do well to remind ourselves that while our approval is enormously important to our children, we should resist attaching our own self-esteem to our children's accomplishments. Instead, we can be proud of helping our kids own their successes and failures without looking to us for the ultimate judgment.

KSB

The Too-Nice Child

Asserting oneself begins at birth. Parents quickly learn to recognize the insistent screams babies make to express, "I'm hungry NOW" or "Something really hurts!" Asserting oneself becomes all too evident during the toddler years when "Me do" and "No" provoke nods from adults who mutter to one another, "the terrible twos."

Although it tries our patience, this strong push toward independence is a predictable part of growing up, and we look forward to the next stage when our child insists on independence in more tolerable ways.

But there are children like 4-year-old Sarah, who always seems to give in to her friends. It seems she often lets another child grab the doll carriage or puzzle she was playing with. And then there is Vince who, uncomplaining, returns to building his block tower after two boys steal some of the blocks he'd gathered to use.

We are often grateful for children who aren't always stomping around insisting on their rights. We tend to label them as "easy going" and "nice." We are grateful for a play date free of fights, but it worries us to see our 4-year-old always give in. We may try to relieve our worry by thinking that our preschooler could be weighing the differences between things that can be ignored and situations that need attention. "She's simply the early version of the adult who doesn't get hyper about little things and decides most things aren't worth a hassle or fuss-up," one father observed while watching his 3-year-old give in to a bully.

Repeated compliant behavior like this should raise a red flag. What was really happening, and how was Sarah feeling as she watched her carriage disappear? It is unrealistic to assume she could make on-the-spot decisions about what's important to pursue and what might not be worth the trouble. At age 3 or even 4, children are unable to think this way. That doll carriage was an important part of Sarah's play, as were Vince's blocks. They had chosen these things to play with, their imaginations were at work, and they had plans in mind. Just because they are so young and "only playing" does not mean the things they have chosen to do are not terribly important to them. Will they continue to give in and be so "nice" when they are 10 years of age and friends urge them to be mean to another friend, or at fifteen when they are offered drugs? Will they be afraid to say "no"?

What's a good way to think about these interactions between 3- and 4-year-olds? We should ask ourselves why they didn't stand up for themselves. Were the other children frightening peers who always become aggressive when they don't get their way? Had they both perhaps received strong messages from adults that nice girls and boys share and keep unhappy feelings to themselves? Perhaps they felt very small, and their feelings of inadequacy were so overwhelming that they were incapable of finding the strength to hold on to the carriage or the blocks and say "No."

We as parents are conflicted as we nurture and teach our children. One of the lessons we work on is helping young children learn to share. We praise them when they don't get upset and let other friends play with their toys. But sharing means taking turns, not giving in, and if we see our 3- or 4-year-old continually relinquishing a toy to another child, we should observe thoughtfully and notice behaviors and expressions.

Did she really want to share her carriage or did she hesitate, appear uncertain and then reluctantly move on to something else? Was Vince looking a little afraid of the other kids?

Some children are frightened at the prospect of showing displeasure or anger so it's important for parents to remain calm. We can reassure our children by telling them it's all right to be angry, particularly when something feels unfair. We can help by giving our children the words to use, such as "No!" or "I was playing with that!"

But the starting point is to understand that a child's play involves some serious developmental business. Children who have feelings of inadequacy or are afraid to stand up for themselves may not make a fuss when a toy they have chosen to play with is suddenly taken away. Sarah and Vince don't know how to make things right for themselves or are afraid to try. Knowing this, we can gently move in beside each of them and help.

MLK

Modesty

The Grandmothers' personal grandchildren are, of course, perfect in every respect. And even if they weren't, the Grandmothers know well the first rule of grandmothering: Offer no advice or criticism except in cases of the most dire emergency.

Nonetheless, the Grandmothers who have adolescent grandkids are sometimes tempted to go wrap a scarf around our teenage granddaughters' upper bodies so as to cover some of that cleavage they seem to be so proud of, or to tug at the hems of those teeny-tiny skirts that barely cover their alluring little behinds. Not to mention the grandsons with their colorful briefs on display. Equally alarming are the outfits worn by the younger grandchildren, just as provocative as those of their older siblings. How can these kids focus on their schoolwork, we wonder, with all that skin and underwear on display? Whatever happened to modesty?

We know, we know—it's the style. It's what's for sale online and on the racks in the shopping malls. It's what everyone else is wearing.

You can stop reading right now if you have no complaint about young people's current tastes in clothing and no worries about your children some day following suit. But if you think that maybe something has been lost in the Facebook era, that nothing at all seems to be private anymore, not even our bodies, read on. Maybe you'd like to start developing your child's fashion sense in a different direction.

Modesty is not prudishness; it is a matter of valuing one's body. Very young children, just out of diapers, start demonstrating a desire for privacy, closing the bathroom door, wanting to dress themselves without onlookers. We need to notice when this happens and, instead of considering it cute and funny, we need to respect this need, to grant them their modesty. Who looks at a child's body should be in his/her control.

Modesty also means that Mom and Dad don't parade their own scantily or not-at-all clothed bodies around the house. At some point as babies grow from toddlers to preschoolers, they are going to start looking at you funny when they see you with no clothes on. That's the time to start covering up and closing doors. There's no need to freak out if your child walks in on you naked, but respond to your child's need for privacy with your own display of modesty.

Why, you ask? Children whose modesty is respected develop self-respect. This self-respect is evidenced in ways that can go far beyond how they dress; it can affect the way they learn, make friends and relate to others. They develop the ability to judge others and choose their friends by their actions and words, not their looks. They learn to feel good about themselves no matter how small they are, or how pudgy, or how light or dark of skin. They are proud enough of their bodies to keep them appropriately covered, not show them off. They are far less likely as they grow older to fall victim to sexual predators, or to text photos of their genitalia to their friends, or send out obscene messages via the Internet.

Do we realize that in some cultures partial or total nudity is not viewed as shocking or even erotic? Indeed we do, but we're talking about *this* culture, where we expect people who expose themselves to be arrested. Do we think our granddaughters and grandsons are on the road to perdition because of the way they dress? Of course not. But we're pretty sure that they could find stylish yet more modest clothing to wear if they made the effort. And we worry that with the current relaxed attitude toward sexuality that pervades the television programs and films they see, they might not realize what messages are conveyed by the way they dress, the texts they send or the Facebook messages they post.

They might think that it has always been this way. But it hasn't. Once there was a quality called modesty. We'd like to see it make a comeback.

KSB

Learning to Use the Potty

Arecent newspaper article reminded us Grandmothers of a perennial problem. The subject was parents' frustration with the requirement of nursery schools and child care centers that 3-year-olds must be out of diapers before they can enroll. It made us wonder how parents could have missed the signs, which usually appear near the end of the second year, that their child is ready to take charge of his body in this way.

Of course, we are equally concerned when parents try to push their child to use the potty when she is too young, when she is not really aware of what her body is doing and how to respond. Before at least 18 months of age, it is rare that a child has the ability to control her muscles or is emotionally ready to use the potty. For a 1-year-old, it's the parent who is "trained," not the child.

Though some parents may begin toilet training before their child is ready, more common are the parents who keep on diapering their kids long past the time when it is appropriate.

They are failing to pick up on signals that their child knows what is going on with his body and is ready to take this next step in his self-care. This awareness comes for most children in the latter part of their second year. But some parents miss the signs that it's time to bring out the potty, usually because they are preoccupied with the many demands of their busy lives.

This seems to be a more common problem nowadays, and one reason may be because parents see that drugstore shelves are lined with boxes of disposable "pull-ups"—not just for little ones, but for kids up to 50 pounds! As a result, parents get a message from the manufacturers of these products that it's normal for 3-year-olds and 4-year-olds to still be wearing diapers.

So how can you know when your child is ready to use the potty and start wearing real cotton underpants? It might help to think of another self-care skill that he or she has already mastered. When, as a baby, your child pushed away the spoon as you tried to feed her, you knew she was ready to be a big girl. You then began providing finger foods and giving her plenty of time to learn how to feed herself. And wasn't she proud!

Now, let's look at some signs that your toddler is ready to take the perfectly natural developmental step of beginning to use the potty. You have surely noticed the signs that he is urinating or having a bowel movement, so you can help him recognize what's going on by asking, "Can you feel that you're pooping? Let me help you use the potty for that." When he wants to avoid all kinds of messes and hates to have dirty hands, it's a sign that he wants to be clean. Maybe he asks to have his diaper changed or notices how pleased you are when he smells so much nicer after the change. When he resists lying down passively to be diapered, you know it's time!

These are all signs that it's time for big boy/big girl underpants—not pull-ups. Pull-ups will just mask the problem. Because the super-absorbent material from which they're made wicks the urine away from kids' bodies, they never feel that uncomfortable, wet feeling that will motivate them to learn to use the toilet.

Now it's time to bring out the potty. If he will be using the toilet, make sure you have a stool under his feet so he doesn't have to worry that he will fall in. Ideally, you will want to begin this learning process at a time when life is relatively calm, with no big changes coming, such as a move, a new baby or new school. It also helps if you aren't too busy yourself to take your child to the toilet whenever he lets you know he needs to go. When you are away from home, you will want to make sure you know where the restrooms are located so you can get him there promptly. It also helps if you can stay as calm as possible when accidents happen, as they surely will.

Be as positive about the whole experience as possible, encouraging your child and letting her know that using the toilet is a big accomplishment—hers, not yours. Offering to reward her with prizes or bribes will make this process more about pleasing you than about gaining mastery of her own body. Her pride in her independence, her pleasure in taking charge of her own body, is the true reward.

Knowing when he needs to use the toilet and then doing so successfully creates a sense of competence in a toddler that will give him the confidence to take on bigger challenges later, at school and in life, with every expectation that he will succeed.

So be on the lookout for the signs that your child knows what her body is doing. Give her the gift of your confidence and your patience as you support her in taking this vital developmental step. You will have given her a tremendous gift— pride in her accomplishments and self-esteem that will last a lifetime.

GTR

Protection from Sexual Predators

News reports of teachers, coaches and child care workers using their positions of trust to take advantage of children have caused all of us to worry about our kids' safety and to wonder how to safeguard them from predators. And while cases of child abuse or abduction by a stranger are extremely rare, we know that this is an area parents are concerned about and need help with.

Of course, parents of school-age children can talk to their kids about speaking up when someone's behavior makes them feel uncomfortable. It is appropriate to help older kids be aware of sexual assault, even if the chance of that occurring is unlikely.

Helping preschoolers protect themselves requires a totally different approach. We caution parents about scaring young children with lectures about the danger of speaking to strangers or the importance of sounding the alarm if they are touched by anyone other than Mommy, Daddy, grandparents or trusted caregivers.

Self-protection is a big responsibility that young kids cannot possibly take on for themselves. It is the job of the adults to ensure that children are always being cared for by someone who has been checked out thoroughly and found to be trustworthy.

Little kids can become utterly confused when parents urge them to protect themselves. They may begin to imagine all kinds of scenarios that make them afraid of going to sleep, of the dark, or of speaking to anyone. They may also become overly excited and begin engaging in sexual play with other children.

But there are ways parents can help young children resist people who would take advantage of them that do not involve talking directly about the subject. Kids learn by observing what their parents do day-in and day-out. They watch how their parents behave with strangers, who they talk to or engage with and who they avoid.

Another way parents can help little children establish safe boundaries is by respecting their natural desire to do things for themselves—things like washing, going to the toilet and getting dressed. Parents should be pleased when their children take that next step of demanding privacy, wanting to dress themselves and use the bathroom without anyone looking on. This is evidence that they are growing up and asserting control over their own bodies. If you can respect their wishes for privacy and recognition that their bodies are theirs to control, you will greatly reduce the chance your child will ever let anyone do something to her that she isn't comfortable with.

Here are some ways you can help your young children develop a sense of self-worth so that they will know when they are being treated disrespectfully and feel entitled to defend themselves.

• Treat kids with as much respect as you do adults, both physically and emotionally.

• Protect them from intrusive behavior by other adults—such as unwanted kisses, hugs, tickling, jokes and teasing.

- Support kids when they say "no" to others or show by their actions that they don't like the way they're being treated.
- Respect your kids' privacy when posting pictures on social media; when they are old enough to give consent, make sure you have it for anything you post about them.
- Help kids find ways to defend themselves when playmates or siblings tease or bully them.
- Respect and support kids' need for control over what gets put into, taken out of and otherwise done to their bodies; insist that doctors and nurses explain what they are about to do—and why—and make sure your child understands and agrees whenever possible.
- Resist the temptation to engage in physical contact that may be overly stimulating to your child or make him feel helpless, such as excessive tickling or horseplay. If someone else is treating your child in this way, step in and stop it.
- Help kids develop a sense of their own personal space.
- Carefully check out any person you leave your child with and take seriously any doubts or hesitations you or your child might have, especially if he or she is showing unusual behavior either when that person is around or in general.
- Pay attention to what kids say and behaviors that show they are upset or confused, and let them know you don't just assume adults or people in authority are always right.

As a society we are becoming more aware of how often people in positions of authority use their power to take advantage of others. The most obvious and egregious instance of this is adults who abuse young children, causing traumatic and long-lasting psychological consequences for them. When we take steps in their early years to instill a solid sense of self-worth and teach them how to avoid or stand up to people who disrespect them, we are helping to make a safer world for everyone.

GTR

PART FIVE

They Crawl Before They Walk

Child Development

The ages and stages of child development that you've read about haven't changed through the years. In your eagerness to see your child excel, don't expect 4-year-old behavior from your 2-year-old. Learn what is "age appropriate" and what is not. That works both ways: try to figure out, for example, why your 4-year-old is acting like a 2-year-old.

Bedtime Struggles

Children who resist bedtime are noted for their determinedly open eyes and loud protests, often at the hour when the caregiver is most desperate for quiet and rest. Unfortunately, such wakefulness is not something that occurs once and then is outgrown forever, but is a stage that can reappear at different ages. The parent's role is not to put the child to sleep but to encourage the child to learn to do this for herself.

The wakeful infant has learned to associate sleep with rocking, feeding or sucking. So when a baby wakes up to discover that he's alone in his crib, not being rocked or fed any more, or that the pacifier has fallen out of his mouth, he can't go back to sleep on his own.

The wakeful toddler has separation anxiety. She wants you by her side even more than she does by day because she feels vulnerable at bedtime, much as you do when concerns that you can handle at 3 p.m. have you staring at the ceiling in the dark at 3 a.m. So when she awakens during the night she tries to lure you back with requests—for a drink, a kiss, one more story—or by insisting that there's a dragon in her closet.

Depending on your own bedtime, you are either irritated that the child is interrupting your adult time with your spouse, a book or a hobby you enjoy, or you are somewhere between tired and exhausted. Your patience is short, but at the same time, you feel guilty over your annoyance, especially if the child spent much of the day in the child care center or with a sitter. So you are tempted to invite her to stay up another hour or to sleep in your bed, where at least you'll be together, she'll be quiet, and you can both get some sleep.

You do both need your sleep, but you also need some child-free hours. And by giving in, you're perpetuating the problem.

To begin solving it, make bedtime as pleasant as possible. Do not rush it, no matter how much of a hurry you are in. Prepare your child with a half-hour warning, and if possible devote that half hour to an activity the child particularly enjoys—a quiet and calming one, of course—giving him your full attention. Then make actual bedtime a pleasurable time of conversation, cuddles, songs and stories. Recorded music, perhaps the same familiar tunes each night, can become signals for sleep. Nightlights can be comforting to children who express a fear of the dark; older children can be permitted to look at books by themselves and turn out their own lights when they are ready. A beloved stuffed animal or special blanket is often helpful in keeping a child content through the night.

But whatever the bedtime props, when it becomes time to say goodnight, say it with conviction. If the child fusses for a while, let him fuss. If he continues, go to him with reassuring words and pats, but not with an invitation to join the grown-ups in front of the TV or in bed. If necessary, sit beside the child's own bed until he is calmed. Assure him that you will keep him safe through the night, and express confidence that soon, possibly tonight, he will be able to fall asleep right away, and sleep until morning.

Trust your own sense of whether your child is protesting bedtime only in the hopes of squeezing a little more activity into his day or if he is truly distressed. Remember your own childhood fears at bedtime, and how vivid they were. If, after your best bedtime performances and your repeated reassurances that all is well, your child is still unable to sleep, consider consultation with a child development specialist. You and your child both may need help in understanding the causes of his persistent wakefulness.

KSB

Toddlers' Anger

We expect our young children to have occasional meltdowns, and usually we manage to handle them well, comforting them through the storm and talking about them afterward, reflecting on how in the future we might want to avoid such tumult. And gradually we hope we can help our children outgrow their tantrums and self-centeredness, becoming kind and well-liked but also able to stick up for themselves.

Sometimes it seems, though, that the look in your toddler's eyes is pure malice and that he would knock you flat if he could. Well, you're right, he would. But rather than turning on him in retaliation because you're bigger than he is, deflect his blows, and remind him not of your size and strength but that he, in fact, really does love you. Eventually his angry feelings will be outweighed by his love for you, which is just as strong as his desire to punch you in the face and in time becomes stronger.

He may still want to injure you, but he won't try to do it, to you nor to his playmates who anger him.

In fact, if you're at all lucky, he'll learn to use his words. Doubtless you've heard your child's patient preschool teacher use this expression, "Use your words!" and maybe some of the children actually know what she means, that rather than knock down someone's block building, far better to tell him what annoyed you.

One wise Hanna Perkins Center therapist we know is teaching children to distinguish between small, medium and big mad feelings. This lesson is for 4- and 5-year-olds, kindergarteners and early elementary school kids, not toddlers, who aren't quite ready to learn such nuances. But when one learns to use one's words, once calmed down a little, one realizes that there's a difference between annoyed, upset and infuriated. OK, maybe the children don't learn those exact words. But they learn to differentiate between the three and to control their urge to hurt someone with actual blows or ugly words.

What words might he learn to use?

"NO!"

"That's mine!"

"I was playing with that!"

"I am mad because I was having a good time playing with that, and you took it away from me!"

"I am mad because I was watching that TV program, and you made me turn it off!"

Or even, "I am mad because you used to play with me, and now you play with that baby all the time!" That one doesn't seem likely, but you might teach him to say those words next time he tries to pinch either you or the baby.

A hard lesson, this one, that your sweet-faced toddler sometimes contemplates assaulting his devoted mom. But remember how at the same time he adores and is entirely dependent on you. Help him learn to remember that love he has for you and also for his siblings and playmates so that he can grow up to be kind.

Kind is more important than anything.

KSB

Discipline: Punishment or Learning?

Helping a child choose right from wrong can be the most important influence a parent can have. A child who has learned to feel good about himself/herself when doing the right thing is more likely to grow into an adult who contributes to the well-being of society. The important issue here is how parents help a child "choose" for herself/himself rather than force a decision. The key is the method of discipline.

The young child lives in the moment, and so natural curiosity and impulsiveness are all it takes to land him in trouble. Most forms of physical punishment, yelling or threatening will stop undesired behavior in its tracks, but there may be little or no carryover of learning into the next similar situation. He doesn't stop to think, "The last time I did that, I was punished, and I don't want that to happen again." At this point, he cannot consider what part he played to cause this effect from you.

Parents usually find that in using the lash-out methods of discipline, the behavior pattern is repeated over and over again and the child never learns. These kinds of punishment often belittle the child and tend to foster more anger and self-pity than reflection. She may grow up feeling that hurting and being hurt are the only ways differences can be resolved. Some children who experience physical or belittling punishment become bullies. They feel important by making others feel scared and helpless. This is why the Grandmothers disapprove of physical and emotional punishment!

The only good thing about "Go to your room!" is that it gives an angry parent a chance to cool down. However, the very young child is often left feeling alone and abandoned with his bad self. Both child and parent may need some space before trying to probe why he misbehaved and what can be done about it, but the very young child needs the presence of the adult to help contain his overwhelming feelings and to be assured he is loved no matter how much he angered his parents. Reading a story, listening to quiet music or doing a puzzle together may help both of them calm down and be more receptive to thoughts about how these bad times can be avoided.

Parents can then talk with the child and appeal to that side of her that wishes to do the right thing. (Yes, believe it or not, every child has that side!). They can help her think about how she doesn't like the "bad girl" feeling about herself. The child could be helped to wonder:

"Wouldn't you rather be the boss of yourself rather than have me get angry and tell you what to do?"

"When you didn't stop yourself from teasing and being wild, you spoiled the fun you were having. Next time, maybe you can stop yourself; then everyone would like being with you more."

"When we tell you that you may not have something or do something you want to do right now, crying and yelling won't make us change our minds. You'll feel much better if you stay calm so we can talk about it. Then we can still have fun together."

By guiding the child in this way, parents can help him think about finding pleasure in resisting the impulses that cause him to get into trouble. This kind of discipline usually has a much more lasting, productive outcome. There are differences, of course, between guiding a toddler and an older child.

Very young toddlers who have just discovered their mobility are in a double bind when it comes to appropriate behavior. They are extremely curious and highly impulsive. Everything is interesting and belongs to them. They need to be watched every minute, but no amount of vigilance can keep them from all mishaps. When their investigations involve doing something unsafe, they must be stopped immediately and firmly, yet calmly. They may rage against this, and removing them from the area is a good first step. Toddlers are not yet ready to understand cause and effect, so explanations will not accomplish much. Diversion is the best tactic. Help them become interested in something else. Let them know through words and facial expressions which things please you and which ones do not. Toddlers take great delight in Mommy's and Daddy's (or their caregivers') smiles and words of approval. They also react with concern when they see your frowns and hear the word "no." Through these interactions, repeated many times, they begin to grasp the concept of cause and effect.

As children grow older and more responsible for their actions, they are able to make more tangible atonements, depending on the seriousness of the infraction. It helps to make the consequence fit the crime. For example: If your child has been destructive with one of his belongings or yours or his friend's, he could be included in its mending or fixing in some small way. If the item cannot be repaired, he could lend his friend something his friend has liked to play with.

If she has been unkind toward a friend, she could dictate and copy a note of apology or color an "I'm sorry" picture.

If she cannot play with her toys in an appropriate, safe way, they could be put out of reach for a while and restored to their proper shelf gradually.

If he tests your limits in public, remain calm but take him home immediately or as soon as you can. When you're home, tell him how disappointed you are that he had to interrupt your outing and how embarrassed he must have been when others saw such a fine boy acting that way. Tell him you hope someday soon he can go with you again and be the big boy you know he wants to be. Children respond well when you appeal to their "growing up" side and when it is noticed and mentioned with approval. Growing up and being able to do "big-girl" and "big-boy" things is their mission in life and a great motivator for learning self-control.

Thoughtful parental discipline offers better pay-offs than angry, in-the-moment responses to bad behavior. The results are longer lasting and carry over from one developmental stage to another. And your hands will not sting from spanking little bottoms, and your voice will not be raspy from ineffective yelling!

GS

Starting Preschool
and Child Care

When parents give over the care of their child to a preschool, child care center or kindergarten teacher, it is an emotionally difficult time for all. Parents tend to stifle their feelings with bravado, telling the child: "There will be a lot of other children for you to play with!" "Look at all the toys and things to do!" "Your teacher will help you learn all sorts of new things!" But when the reality of leaving comes, this encouragement usually cannot make up for the abandonment the child feels nor the parents' anxiety.

The personnel of some schools and centers believe that the best way for the child to handle this difficult time is to encourage her to "forget" Mommy and Daddy while there. They may try to divert the child with activities and materials. But, children asked to sit on these feelings often react with negative or debilitating behavior such as withdrawal, destructiveness or being hurtful to others. In more forward-looking schools, the teachers and caregivers know that asking young children to give up thinking about Mommy and Daddy is like asking them to give up pieces of themselves. They help children find ways to keep parents in mind, to serve as a source of strength and comfort even if they are not with them. If this is not part of the intake process for your choice of center (it should be!), we hope you will insist or consider another choice if possible.

Hopefully, your child and one or both parents can have a short visit at the center with the teacher or caregiver before her first day. Also, short, planned visits to the center with her and one or both parents during the early "settling in" time may be very helpful. The visit could be to have lunch or to do one or two activities with her. Having lunch, doing a puzzle, building a Lego or block construction puts Mom's and Dad's seal of approval on their child's new world. It will also provide a memory of togetherness the next time their child engages in these activities.

To help your child when you're not there, take a picture of you with him to keep in his backpack or cubby at school. During stressful times, he can use the picture to comfort himself and to remember that Mommy and Daddy are missing him, too. Include a short note (perhaps a new one every few days), telling the child that Mommy and Daddy are thinking of him and will be so proud when they hear about all the things he did that day. Teachers can use these notes when the child's feelings distract him from activities.

The very young child can use a personal item—Mom's or Dad's old billfold, scarf, piece of jewelry—to stand in for them. Just knowing that the object is in her backpack, coat pocket or cubby to be checked on or touched occasionally (not played with) can be comforting.

Some parents make a stick-figure booklet with simple captions depicting the tasks they'll be doing at their workplace or home during the day. If the teacher notices that the child's attention or self-control is waning, this booklet can be read with her so that she can picture her parents doing their work as she does hers.

If the early separation time is particularly difficult for a child, or if he is experiencing more stress from things going on in his home life, an arranged phone call to him can help. This should be talked over and planned with the teacher. Initially, the sound of a parent's voice on the phone may cause tears. This is all part of the process of experiencing "missing" feelings and, with help, learning that they can be managed. When the child no longer needs these reinforcements, his mastery of anxiety can be a source of pride and a sign of becoming a "big boy."

If the school or center cannot or prefers not to fulfill such requests, it's best not to make an issue of it. Perhaps after the staff sees how comforting it is to your child when you are considerate of and talk about missing feelings, they may be more responsive to those requests they can manage.

When parents talk over the child's day when they are reunited, they can make a plan for what the child can do the next day when she feels lonely, angry, sad or frustrated. They can preface the plan by saying, "If you feel that way again, you can tell yourself what Mommy or Daddy would do or say if they were there—then you'll be able to do it for yourself." This calls upon the "growing-up" side of the child, using thoughts of Mom and Dad's words of support to feel less helpless, to take charge of herself and move on. If the caregiver or teacher is aware of this plan, he or she can use it to advantage, asking the child, "What would Mom or Dad say or do when such-and-such happens?"

When the child feels that her parents and her teacher are partners on her behalf, that her parents like and respect the teacher, it paves the way for the teacher to become someone who helps her learn new things. The child will be better able to enjoy learning and new relationships.

GS

Staying Connected

Alyssa's mom stuffed her uniform into her locker, picked up her coat and purse and quickly ran to her car. She didn't want to be late picking up her 3-year old daughter from her child care center.

When Mom came into the room, Alyssa ran to her and became whiny and clingy, saying, "Mommy, pick me up, pick me up." Mom picked her up and held her close. Alyssa's teacher walked up to them and said, "She really had a very good day except for nap time." Mom put her down and told her she'd help her put on her coat (this wasn't the time to urge her to be a big girl and do it herself) so that they could hurry to the grocery to pick up some milk and a couple of other things for dinner.

In the car, Alyssa snuggled up close to Mommy as she was fastened into the car seat and pouted, "I want to go right home! I don't want to stop at the store!" Her mom patted her, told her it wouldn't take long and that she'd get her a juice box as soon as they got to the grocery.

When Mom tried to lift Alyssa into the shopping cart seat, she stiffened her legs and whined, "Carry me." Mom told her, "I'll carry you to the juice box aisle and then you'll have to sit in the cart seat while you choose which flavor you want." When they got to the juice boxes, Alyssa took a long time to choose the flavor she wanted and finally settled down into the cart seat.

As they headed toward the dairy aisle, Mom's cell phone rang—it was a call from a friend who had left a message just before Mom left work and was calling again. For a few minutes, as she looked for the milk she wanted, she talked with her friend who seemed to just want to chat. As she leaned over to put it in the cart, still listening to her friend on the phone, Alyssa lifted her arms up toward her Mom and whined, "Carry me!" Mom got the message and said to her friend, "I have to go—Alyssa needs me."

Truer words were never spoken. At this point all of Alyssa's emotional reserves for being able to be away from Mom had been used up. Even though she'd had an involved, productive day at her center, seeing Mom at pick-up time opened up a floodgate of missing feelings.

It might seem to some that this mom is coddling or giving in to her whining child. But, she's not. Under these circumstances, she is actually following her good instincts. Because of her connection with her child's feelings, she can sense Alyssa's need for her attention. She can feel that Alyssa's coping energies for being away from home and Mom all day are all used up. Just giving Alyssa this fifteen-minute "recharge" every day makes all the difference in how the evening goes.

A mother nurtures her baby before she is born and continues to, even though she no longer has the same kind of physical connection. As her mother gazes at and talks with her infant as she tends to her needs, the baby soon recognizes and distinguishes her mother's face and voice from others. She soon knows the distinctive feel and scent of her mother's body as she cradles her when she picks up her baby. This makes the infant feel connected and secure.

As the baby grows into a toddler, then a 3-year old, this feeling of safety and connectedness helps her be able to make new relationships and take in new experiences. Mrs. Erna Furman, the child development consultant from whom the Grannies learned so much, used to say, "A mother has to be there (be connected with) to be left." In other words, still feeling her mother's connection with her helps the growing child to reach out and expand her world.

There are so many distractions and demands for mothers these days. It is often impossible to respond to mothering instincts in the moment, even for a stay-at-home mom. She may have a wide range of obligations. She may be responsible for an older family member's care-giving. She often chauffeurs her kids to their after-school activities. Often she is involved in community affairs and their meetings.

It is especially hard for moms who work because they're wearing two hats. Alyssa's mom likes her job, and the family could surely use the extra money. She likes her co-workers and feels stimulated when working with adults even though she is often exhausted at the end of the day. At times, though, she feels guilty, especially at Alyssa's pick-up time, that she might be short-changing her child. Often, she thinks about the experiences Alyssa has that she isn't a part of. Her feelings waft back and forth with all of these times of leaving and picking up. Even though she wouldn't change it for the world, she can't help thinking, "Being this important to my little girl can sometimes be a pretty hard job!" And it is. However, Alyssa is learning something valuable, too—being able to wait and enjoy activities without Mom being at her side and able to draw on her own resources because she can feel connected to Mom "inside."

Before Alyssa's first day at the center, Mom and Dad had both visited so they could tell Alyssa about it. Then Mom and Alyssa visited and participated in some of the activities together. On her first day there on her own, she had given a picture of Mom, Dad and Alyssa to tape in her cubby to look at when she was missing Mom and Dad. She also gave her one of her scarves and one of Dad's T-shirts to hold when she felt lonely at nap time. That way, she could feel her Mom and Dad with her.

In time, little ones won't need as much attention to feel connected and secure. Their horizons will have widened to include people other than those of their immediate family. All too soon it will seem a clingy, dependent young child will become an independent teenager who often acts as though she doesn't know you!

GS

Readiness for "School" Learning

At one time, kindergarten readiness meant knowing one's name, address and phone number, being able to print one's name, counting up to a certain number, reciting letters of the alphabet in order—and in those days, tying one's shoes! These are helpful accomplishments but in reality have little to do with readiness for learning in a school setting. In the past, kindergarten was the first school program most children attended. In today's world, many under-fives have been enrolled in child care or preschool programs. Even so, at this young age, they may again experience some of the same anxieties or worries as they did when they first started a program away from home.

Parents have been their child's first teachers from the moment he/she was born and have all of the requirements needed to have him/her ready and eager to learn in a different environment and from other people. No special kits, flashcards or materials hyped in TV ads are necessary! In the everyday life as a family, parents guide their children through many milestones they should accomplish to help them be school-ready.

Even the most intellectually gifted children need to have mastered certain developmental tasks in order to take in new learning, using it productively and with pleasure.

Self-Care: You won't be with him or her to take care of bodily needs (eating, toileting, dressing, wanting to be clean); it will be up to him. So, take advantage as he shows signs of wanting to "do it myself." As he tries to be more independent, you can encourage each small step and admire his efforts. A child who can do for himself in a new environment can be less dependent on others, freer to focus on taking in and using new concepts.

Communication: Your child will be ready for school when he can tell others what he needs, when he needs help and what he doesn't understand. Encourage him to use words at home to let you know what he wants and how he feels. Try to find time to have conversations with your growing-up child so that he is used to using his words and listening to others. Help him put into words how he feels when he looks sad or acts angry. When he is curious about his world and asks questions, try to take the time to answer him simply. His "Why?" and "What's a. . .?" curiosity will make him an eager learner at school. The ability to communicate at school will keep the learning tasks focused and not sidetracked into interfering behaviors of acting out or shutting down because of the frustration of not understanding or not being understood.

Being Part of a Group: Being able to play comfortably with others her age will help greatly when she is at school with a number of other children. As you observe your child playing with others, watch for her ability to wait for a turn and share materials. If she has difficulty, help her see that the fun she was having was spoiled because she made her playmate feel bad by taking away something he was using, because she pushed in front of him, because she wouldn't share. Help her want to be liked and to see her role and responsibility for whether things go well and if she and her friends are having fun. Help her see that when she is mean or destructive, she spoils the play. When she can use more inner controls to behave in a friendly way rather than always needing outer discipline, she will feel good about herself and have more positive energy for learning and making good relationships.

Missing Feelings: Missing Dad, Mom and home feelings are normal but do not need to overwhelm your child. Point out to him all of the things he can already do on his own because he worked hard and practiced. Tell him how proud you are of all the ways he shows you that he is growing up. Let him know that you will be missing him, too, but that his school is a place you know about and like. Try to plan a visit to the school, see his room and meet his teacher before the starting day. If he has seen his room and met his teacher with you, it serves to put your stamp of approval on it and he can feel that he is safe.

When you do visit his room, you can point out some of the activities he is already familiar with, such as the blocks, puzzles and the art materials. Remembering these things he did at home with you will help him be able to do activities at school when you're not with him. This will be an indication that your child is becoming a person unto himself. His teacher then can do what a teacher is meant to do—be the child's guide and partner in activities and learning.

There may be setbacks. Even though he may have been in other programs, this transition is different and may recall missing feelings again. At home, be prepared to listen and give your child the opportunity to express the worries and frustrations he or she may have. Admire the way he could tell you and let you help with his feelings. Let him know you have missed him, too, but feel so proud of all the good growing up he's shown he can do. The more confidence you have in him, the more confident he can be.

GS

Lying

If your once totally trustworthy 5-year-old has started telling fibs, she or he is right on schedule. Five is the age at which many children not only begin to shade the truth to protect themselves from possible punishment but also make up stories that they insist are real for no apparent reason.

We all, adults and children alike, try to avoid admitting to mistakes and misdeeds. Young children just aren't as sophisticated in hiding their tracks. They will swear that they didn't spill the milk while standing in a puddle of white with an empty carton in their hands. In those situations, when there's no doubt in our minds that they are lying, we can say, "I'm sure you wish you hadn't spilled the milk, but accidents do happen, to all of us. Let's clean it up together, and I know you'll feel better." The child already feels guilty and doesn't need to be lectured about telling the truth.

Maybe later, or while cleaning up, you can talk about how

she felt when she sensed the milk slipping from her hands and why she said what she did. You can reassure her that you love her no matter what and you're sorry you yelled at her the last time she spilled something. You don't want your tone or your punishments to be so harsh that she's afraid to tell the truth once she's old enough to know the difference between what she wished had happened and what actually did.

But what if she denies doing something you didn't observe, such as hitting a sibling? What if little toddler sister comes into the room crying and pointing a finger with big 5-year-old sister right behind her, denying having so much as touched her? Don't jump to conclusions. Comfort the smaller sister, and say to the larger one, "It's not important that *I* know whether you hit her; it's important that *you* know. You'll feel bad if you really did hit her and you don't try to make it up to her somehow."

She will feel relieved, in fact, if and when she owns up to having given her sister a couple of furtive smacks. That will feel so much better than being left with a sense of dread that she won't be able to fool you for long, that her crime will be discovered. After a quick confession she'll be able to make things right again and go about with a clear conscience. Your role in this is getting her to respect that conscience, rather than depend on you for approval or disapproval.

Then there are the tall tales. What a thrill to be able to dupe the grown-ups! A small person can feel big, important and powerful by relating her fantasies as if they were real; for example, in telling the adults that her kindergarten teacher brought her pet camel to school when really it was a chameleon, and that everyone got to ride it around the playground. Again, there is no cause for demanding that the absolute truth be told. You might say something like, "Wouldn't that have been fun, to ride a camel? I liked that story!" Later, at bedtime maybe, you might ask, "What did your teacher *really* bring to school?" and then have a conversation about real and pretend. Or you just might let it go and enjoy your kid's emerging sense of humor and imagination.

The thing to keep in mind here is what's in the child's best interests, not whether she's offended your moral standards. So don't push her into telling lie upon lie by trying to force her to admit that she did, in fact, spill the milk. Remember what they say: A lie told often enough eventually is believed as the truth, even by the liar.

Instead, try to model honesty for your children. You might avoid telling them to lie about their ages so they can get reduced fares, for example, or asking them to answer the phone and tell the caller that you're not at home.

A 5-year-old's fresh, new conscience is very hard on her sometimes, so it's no wonder she's quick to deny any wrongdoing. She's also at the age where she's discovering that fantasy is not reality and that wishes do not necessarily come true, and she is experimenting with this new knowledge. Put away the polygraph and simply help her to learn the difference.

KSB

Tattling

Five-year-old Mindy's continual tattling is becoming a real pain. Although you're pleased that she is well-behaved and rule-conscious, she seems to take such pleasure in telling on others. "Jason didn't finish his milk." "Patty didn't hang up her jacket." And so on. Once again you tell Mindy that it's your job to do the reminding and that when Jason and Patty slip up, it's not the end of the world. Her job is to think about what is right for her to do. You've been through this scenario many times with her, but she seems all the more determined to call your attention to others' misdeeds.

Take heart—tattling is not that unusual for both boys and girls her age and it won't last forever. The 5- and 6-year-old is just beginning to know right from wrong and how not to act on impulse as younger children do. When your tattler was two, you could say "No!" and "Don't" all day, but his natural curiosity and impulsiveness would be saying, "Yes!" and "Do!"

That's why you locked up the bleach and didn't let him play in the backyard all by himself, even if there was a fence around it.

Now that she's older, she can remember and follow the rules better, but there are times when she gives into temptation and knows she shouldn't. She is experiencing the first stirrings of conscience, and sometimes it's confusing. When he tries to ignore this feeling, he is uncomfortable. When he is unable to ignore it and gives into doing what he knows he shouldn't, he feels awful, even guilty.

Guilt is a new feeling, hard to bear, and your child would like to get rid of it. Her conscience is telling her that she needs to be more thoughtful and responsible for the things she does. So now, not only will her parents be telling her what to do, but also this new feeling she doesn't quite understand will be bugging her, too!

It's always easier to point a finger at someone than to feel that she's done wrong. "See, other people break the rules, too." Like recent converts, she's a stickler for the rules. She delights in pointing out other people's transgressions, even those of her parents. In the car with Mom, she reminds her of the "rules of the road." "You didn't stop at that last stop sign!" She calls Dad on the carpet when he lets out an occasional "damn it!"

Her parents need to let her know they understand about those feelings of wanting to rigidly follow the rules and that it is important to have them. You can explain that they could keep her out of trouble. These feelings of "should I" or "shouldn't I" aren't being mean or accusing her but rather are good reminders that help her be the fine girl she'd like to be. You can explain that tattling on others to cover up will never make her feel excused for her misdeeds, and it might only make others angry with her. This is an important phase in her development and will affect her decisions from now on.

GS

Wishful Thinking

Children eagerly anticipate their birthdays for almost the entire year until the wished-for day arrives. When asked, they don't give their age as merely four. No, they tell you they are "four and a half" or "four and three-quarters" until they have finally arrived at five. They have no doubt been expressing their birthday wishes all this while in terms of the gifts they would like to receive and whom they plan to invite to their birthday party, but they may have other wishes, too, that go beyond their anticipation of cake and ice cream.

They may well expect that on that magical day they will become transformed into much bigger people capable of wonders they couldn't perform when they were a mere three or four. A child may imagine that although she cannot roller skate or ride a bike before her birthday, she will be instantly able to skate gracefully, to wheel about on her bike with ease when she achieves her new age. She may ask for a bicycle or roller skates for that very reason and then be crushed when she only falls to the ground, still small and helpless instead of big and powerful as she had fantasized.

Children may even be imagining that they are expected by others to be suddenly big and clever and capable on their birthdays and feel embarrassed when the day comes and goes and they are unchanged. Adults feed into this fantasy by assuring children that, for example, when they are five they will be old enough to go to school, forgetting how literal-minded young children can be. Having heard that message for so many months and years, children might naturally suppose that they will be admitted to kindergarten promptly on their birthdays. (A child might also be anxious about being expected to immediately measure up to all the 5-year-olds he sees going to kindergarten at the moment he, too, has attained that advanced age.)

Obviously more preparation, more thoughtful discussion is needed to assure children that they are indeed growing and learning and achieving, but that the numbers aren't what make it happen. We can look at photos together of when the child was smaller and remember together all the marvelous things she has learned to do since infancy. We can assure the child that she is just as big and accomplished as a 3- or 4- or 5-year-old should be, and that it takes time to learn to roller skate, to ride a bike, but indeed she will learn, just as she is learning to get her shoes on the right feet, to bounce and catch a ball, to pour without spilling.

Children's biggest wish is to be "big." They can't wait until they grow up and have control over things. We see them managing this wish through their imaginative play—pretending to be grown up, to be Superman—but that helps only temporarily. Coping with the wish by working at growing up, by taking pleasure in being in control of oneself, managing dressing, putting toys back where they belong, handling feelings, has a significantly lasting impact on self-esteem.

We can help our children not only by helping them sort out

fantasy from reality but also by encouraging and commenting on these growing-up behaviors as they emerge.

By emphasizing small accomplishments day by day instead of letting our children set their sights on one day of days, we have a better chance of making each birthday a truly happy one.

KSB

Sharing and Apologizing

You may be growing weary of reading here about all the things the Grandmothers want you to remember to do as you raise young children in these uncertain times. We tell you to relax and follow your instincts, except then we add that perhaps your instincts have failed to remind you of quite a number of things, especially in regards to toddlers. Now here comes something else to add to the list—in fact, two other somethings. But in this case we're not saying do, but don't.

Your instincts as a good parent are telling you that your toddler won't have any friends if she doesn't learn to share her toys and apologize for hitting her playmates in the head with them. You want her to grow up to be a generous, caring person who happily gives to others and is awash in regret if she inadvertently hurts someone. You are embarrassed, in fact, when your sweet little toddler hugs to her chest as many of the toys as she can, refusing to share them, and then kicks viciously with a spare foot if a playmate comes near them. She furthermore won't apologize for her, shall we say, unfriendly behavior. You are inclined to shout, "Share!" and "Apologize!" at her with disappointing and increasingly embarrassing results.

We have actually come to set your minds at ease. Your instincts are good, but your timing is off. Your child is a toddler, so your expectations are a little premature. A young child cannot be expected to share. Come to think of it, there aren't very many adults who excel at sharing, either. But a toddler cannot possibly see something from another's point of view, so he has no understanding whatsoever when someone insists that his playmate wants his favorite doll. Yes, of course you want him to *learn* to share, to become a generous human being, but the toddler years are much too soon for that. Telling him to take turns similarly has no meaning to him because he has no sense of time. So what you do when there is one doll but two toddlers is distract your child with another toy or an animal cracker. He can only be generous when he grows to understand that other people have wants and needs, when he is old enough to want to have friends more than he wants every toy to be his and only his. So give yourself and your child a break and stop telling him to share.

Next we have apologizing. See the previous paragraph about toddlers' lack of empathy for others. If she has hurt someone, she can see that they are crying, but she has no sense of regret or shame, nor should we expect her to. Our role is not to be embarrassed in her behalf and shout, "Apologize!" Instead we comfort the injured child and later, much later, if at all, give our kid the chance to make amends somehow. You'll see in your child's eyes any inkling of confusion over the episode and maybe the desire to give the playmate a hug. Or maybe not. The ability to feel remorse comes later, too, so relax and stop demanding apologies.

All we're saying here is bite your tongue when you're tempted to shout "Share!" or "Apologize!" Neither of these admonitions works well with toddlers. They're not being contrary, they're just being the totally self-centered little people that they are. Give them a few months and then start gently suggesting what one might do, rather than grabbing and kicking, in order to have friends.

KSB

PART SIX

Only Once a Child

There's No Do-Over in Childhood

Give your children their entire childhood to do all their growing. They won't get another crack at it. Let them play! Let them make mistakes and learn from them! Let us Grandmothers throw in a few more words of knowledgeable and insightful advice, just because our children never asked us for any!

Slow Down, Parents

It happens every time you go out in public: Old ladies cluck over your adorable children and sigh, "They grow up so fast; before you know it they'll be grown and gone."

It's one of those great truths that old people know but young people find so hard to believe: The child-rearing phase of life won't last forever; in fact, it will be over before you know it. To the new parent just setting out on the journey of child raising, the two decades that lie ahead may seem a daunting mountain to climb. Given the greater longevity people can expect today, this phase is only a small percentage of your total life span. But what an important one!

"The days are long but the years are short" is a phrase that captures this contradictory quality of time. We Grandmothers remember how overburdened, agitated and sleep-deprived we felt when we were raising kids, and that was back in the days before technology. When you add in all the pressure from our overzealous child-rearing culture, the "fear of missing out" that afflicts users of social media, and a steady stream of distractions from our information- and entertainment-mad society, it's no wonder a parent's life today is so stressful.

We may not be up on the latest trends or scientific breakthroughs, but our long-view perspective on life may have other and perhaps greater value. As an old saying goes, "What the elders see while sitting, the young ones standing on their toes won't see." And what we see from where we sit is that the best thing you can do for your kids is to slow down and be fully present in their lives.

You can get a sense of this bigger picture by thinking back to your own most cherished memories from childhood. Perhaps this will help you see what is really important for you to provide for your kids now. Try to imagine what they will recall of these fleeting but formative years.

Here's a useful exercise: Make a list of all the things you could possibly do for a holiday season or during those oh-so-brief days of summer. Then go back over it with a red pencil, striking out everything that is not absolutely essential. With such a simplified list, you can relax and enjoy doing those few key things so that the overriding experience (and the memory your children will take away) will be one of calmness and genuine family togetherness. Of course the most crucial factor for creating such good times will be Mom and Dad's mood and state of mind: Were they happy or mad? Rested or exhausted? Grumpy or joyful? If you are stressed or overly busy, it's unlikely the experience will become a memory your child cherishes and wishes to recall.

One of the Grandmothers thinks back to a Christmas that could have been a disaster but turned into one of her favorite memories from the child-raising years. Her husband's firm had gone out of business just before Thanksgiving, so the plans for

Christmas had to be scaled back drastically. But even though there were no gifts to speak of, the celebration could not have been merrier: They had a tree, they had a feast, they went to church, they had a warm fire and enjoyed playing charades together. With no Christmas shopping to do and no fancy parties or excursions to plan, this young mother felt more rested and relaxed than she had ever felt at Christmastime. That was an extreme situation, but it did help the family focus on what was truly important. It created good memories for all.

Young parents receive all kinds of advice on how to reduce their stress, so we will keep this brief and to-the-point. To simplify and enhance the quality of your life, we suggest you prioritize the following:

Make a point of spending time with the family. Have dinner together as often as possible. At least once a day, really tune in and listen to your child when she is telling you something. If she is shocked and amazed to have your undivided attention, that should tell you something about where your priorities have (or have not) been. And of course, be sure to make time for your spouse every day. This not only sets a wonderful example for the kids but also will help create a more nurturing atmosphere in the home.

Tune into nature as often as possible. Take a moment to notice and appreciate a beautiful sunset or a flock of birds on your way to work or as you are taking the kids to school. Spend time in nature on your own and with your kids. Start noticing the phases of the moon, the changing of the seasons, the activities of the animals in your neighborhood. All these things will help you see beyond our hectic modern culture to the timeless rhythms of the natural world.

Make time for friends and other relationships; having positive people in your life is the best way to protect yourself from stress. Our relationships help us deal with the ups and downs of life and make us feel good about ourselves. And if the friends you have don't make you feel good about yourself, find some who do.

Be realistic in your expectations of yourself and your kids. There is no such thing as a perfect parent who can raise perfect children and make everyone's lives memorable. Take it from the Grandmothers: It can't be done, nor should it be. Instead, strive to be a "good-enough parent."

When you find yourself getting stressed out and frantic under all of the demands placed upon you, ask yourself, "What would the Grandmothers say?" We would say, "Relax, you're good enough. Be kind to yourself. Parenting is a marathon, not a sprint. Pace yourself and slow down." It's the hardest job you will ever have, but also the most enjoyable and meaningful one.

GTR

Not Enough of Mom

Dear Grandmothers,

Up until recently I have been a stay-at-home mom. Then when my husband's pay was cut, I took on a part-time job. My kids (six and eight) are unhappy because I don't spend as much time with them as I used to, but I have to keep this job. Any advice?

—Distraught Mom

Dear Distraught Mom,

We grandmothers claim to know almost all there is to know about raising kids, but your question leads us first to a confession: When we were young mothers, we didn't have to deal with your problem. Remember the '50s? Well, probably you don't, but you've seen it on TV: Very few moms worked; they were at home baking cookies and playing with the kids. Except the truth of the matter is, we didn't play with the kids all that much; the kids entertained themselves for the most part. And some of us got tired of baking cookies and wished we had jobs so we'd have our own bank accounts. The good old days.

But your children won't be comforted much by watching reruns of "Leave It to Beaver." They expect to have as much of your attention as they ever did, and they quite legitimately resent having to share you with your job. Being a modern mom, you probably *did* frequently bake cookies and play with your kids, and now you can't do that as often. What many parents feel in this situation is guilt, so what they say are things like, "I have to work so we can buy [brand name] video games and [brand name] tennis shoes and eat out regularly at the [brand name] hamburger emporium. And won't we have fun at Disneyland this summer?" Parents don't like to disappoint their children, and they don't want to hear about their children's unhappiness. So they try to jolly the kids out of it.

In a word, don't. Instead, acknowledge in full their anger. Try to find out all the specifics of their resentment, and don't try to convince them that they're exaggerating, that it isn't so bad as all that. You don't have to agree, just listen and nod. Tell them that you miss having things the way they were, too. Swallow your guilt and listen to their sadness. Just feeling heard by you will make them feel better, the same way you feel better after having confided your problems to a friend who is a good listener.

Then start talking about ways you all might adjust to this new reality. They don't need to hear the details of the electric bill being overdue and the car needing a new transmission, but you can talk about being a family and working together differently now. Recognize your children for managing to solve a problem or do a task without your help that in the past they might have asked you to do. Emphasize how capable they have become; tell them that, in fact, their help would be appreciated with some of the household tasks that you used to do all by yourself. Explain how you could be spending more time with them if you were doing some of these tasks together; while you're working at the kitchen laptop, for example, they could be helping you get dinner on the table. They could certainly learn to help with the laundry and assist in clean-up after dinner. They might whine from time to time about their newly assigned chores, but you could end up feeling less pressured, they more competent and needed, and all of you important members of the family team.

Explain how their helping frees you up for family play times, and even if it doesn't quite work out that way, be sure to schedule some, for all of your sakes. Don't make these costly outings that you can't really afford, but research some inexpensive or even free activities: The zoo charges no admission on Mondays (in our city, anyway); hikes in the woods on a sunny, snowy day are free; a favorite family board or card game is likewise.

During one of those hikes you might tell your kids about that job of yours and how sometimes you don't like it but often you do, just like sometimes they hate school but often they actually have fun there. Tell them what exactly your work entails, and what you had to learn to be able to do it in words they can understand—and branch off to a discussion of the kind of work they might want to do some day. We want them, after all, to appreciate the world of work, and look forward to it.

You don't have to tell your kids this part, but you could help yourself feel less guilty by realizing that you're actually teaching your children some valuable lifelong lessons here. Although life can be hard, we can usually find ways to cope. If children learn this as they grow up, they will be better prepared for the challenges they meet later on. And you and your husband are setting a wonderful example for your children by working hard together to do what needs to be done, without blaming anyone, without resentment. (Try to voice your blame and resentment only to each other, after the kids are in bed.)

Someday *these* will be the good old days.

KSB

Santa Claus in Moderation

No parent we know takes great pains to protect the true identity of the Tooth Fairy. Maybe that's because by the time a child starts losing teeth—at about six—he's already well aware that there's no good reason for someone in a tutu with wings and a wand to go flitting from bedroom to bedroom gathering up the baby teeth from the world's first-graders. What could she possibly do with them all? Then to confirm his suspicions, you wake him up in the middle of the night feeling around under his pillow, or you forget altogether until he reminds you. But he doesn't complain; he's happy for the extra cash and he enjoys the game.

That a rabbit would hop about carrying a basket and delivering jelly beans is a story so silly that a very small child can see through it. She loves the fantasy of it, however, as well as all that candy that she's actually allowed to eat before breakfast on Easter morning. It wouldn't ruin her day at all if she were to catch you hiding the eggs.

But then there's Santa Claus.

At one extreme are those who, for religious, moral or psychological reasons, abhor this character. He represents greed, they say, not the true spirit of Christmas. He doesn't deserve the credit that he takes from parents who make or buy the gifts. He compels parents to spin lie after lie about how he gets into the house even though they don't have a fireplace, or why he appears in every store and on every street corner, and of course how he can manage to visit millions of homes around the world in only one night. We should tell our children he doesn't exist, these critics say, the earlier the better.

At the other end of the spectrum are parents who seem to want to keep believing in Santa themselves. They tell their kids that Santa "sees them when they're sleeping and knows when they're awake" so they'd better behave or Santa won't leave them any presents. They start decorating the house with red-suited icons shortly after Halloween, insist that their kids visit a department-store Santa and sit on his lap even if they scream in protest, and maintain the Santa myth until their kids are well into elementary school.

Which way to lean on the issue of Santa is up to the individual family, of course, but our recommendation would be for moderation. The fun about believing in Santa is not lost when the pretend aspect of it is acknowledged. It's probably a good idea not to frighten your children with Santa, either with his ability to know if they ate all their peas or fed them to the dog, or by forcing your little one to sit on the lap of someone she never met and doesn't care to. But go ahead and play the game.

Pretend along with your child that there really is a sleigh pulled by reindeer and a North Pole where elves create shiny toys, but you needn't lie and connive to perpetuate the myth. Pretend that Santa brings gifts to your house on Christmas Eve, but if you've spent many hours building a dollhouse or saved up for months in order to buy that special bicycle, let your child know that those gifts are from you. Speculate with your child about how Santa manages to do all those miraculous things, but don't be afraid to explain that it's all make-believe, like the Tooth Fairy and Easter Bunny. Very real, but still pretend. Who knows better than a child about pretending?

And don't keep all the fun for yourself. Let him pretend to be Santa, too.

KSB

Go Outdoors

One of the Grandmothers remembers when parents wrapped their infants up in warm coats, hats and blankets, bundled them into "prams" and wheeled them out into the snowy backyard. Getting fresh air was important. It happened! She has seen the old photos! As a mother in her twenties, urging the kids to go outdoors meant she would get a break from having them underfoot. Later on, when she taught teachers of young children, her students wrote about getting the kids outside to "blow off steam." While all these reasons for going outside were valid, we seldom thought about the valuable learning opportunities children were being exposed to in the natural world. Playing outside is so much more than blowing off steam or giving an adult a break.

It's common knowledge that young children are wired to move and are driven to try new things, explore their ever-more-complicated abilities to better understand their world. They need time, space and the freedom to learn, and they push in every possible way to respond to this basic drive by continuously exercising their bodies, their voices, noses, eyes and ears. When confined to indoor spaces they often drive adults crazy, either by the noise and constant movement or, today, by the invasion of technologies and the amount of time they spend on their iPads and iPhones.

But exactly why is being outside so important? Why are we urging parents to get children outdoors in addition to the idea that they are getting the healthful benefits of fresh air?

Outdoors, in nature, there is no ceiling and no restraining walls. Movement is only inhibited by a child's developmental age or ability. They can learn and challenge their limits by freely exploring the strengths and abilities of their bodies. With no walls, the distance a child's eye can see is no longer restricted but is exercised multiple times as it focuses and refocuses to see at different distances. The exuberant voice of a preschooler, amplified by closed-in spaces and frequently shushed by others in a room, can sing fully when the sky's the limit. Our outdoor world is three-dimensional and has every shape imaginable. The colors of outdoors are more varied than any Crayola box of 64 colors and can repeatedly change with distance, temperature, time of day, or seasonal angle of the sun. Outside is rich in smells whether in the city, the park or the countryside, and smell is one of the most powerful senses associated with learning and memory. The natural textures, available to small hands and feet that love to touch, are limitless. All these experiences, using all the senses, feed the brain more powerfully than the sights, sounds and smells inside.

So, having made a case for going outdoors, parents ask, "But how do we fit going outdoors into our busy work schedules, the maintenance of a home, and now, dealing with the fear of what lurks out there in our neighborhoods, our parks and in the woods?"

The Grandmothers realize the world is different than the world of their growing-up years. The population has expanded, and engineering technology has developed sophisticated communication systems so that we are immediately aware of and frightened by any dreadful thing happening locally or worldwide. Concerns about safety have naturally influenced how parents focus on protecting their kids, and they are cautious about their kids playing outside in groups—much less alone.

We've said being outdoors is beneficial for kids, but we're adding that it's also good for parents and grandparents. Our advice is to go with them! We can all benefit from a walk, filling our lungs with fresh air, and taking time away from work to see a world beyond our desks or computers. Kids will love it as you walk and notice the things that fascinate them . . . as you watch your toddler find a thousand things to stop and examine . . . as you add the latest find to the small bag you've brought along—the acorn, dried worm, small stick or stone. Remember each has its own weight, texture, temperature and color. In each there is so much more learning than from the two-dimensional picture of a stone or an acorn on the iPad screen.

A good idea is to ask a friend and her kids to walk with you to a place where kids can run and play together while you sit and talk. Children thrive in situations in which they are safe, enjoying themselves, planning their play, and knowing their parents are enjoying themselves as well. A few sandwiches in a bag, to be eaten in the park, can extend the outdoor hours, summer or winter, and your children will always find things to do if you're relaxed and enjoying yourself. Be sure you're dressed as warmly as you've dressed them. Try not to be in a hurry.

Because of the increased demands of home and work, we all need to regularly plan to be outdoors with children rather than thinking of it as something we don't have time for. Recognizing not only the benefits to children's health but the valuable lessons the outdoors can teach makes planning outdoor time just as important as any other activity.

We Grandmothers believe that if outside time in our natural world is experienced in the early years, children will develop an emotional attachment to these events. Also, the sights, sounds, smells and the stretching of their bodies will be powerfully remembered and become a huge part of who they grow up to be. They will carry an appreciation and respect for their natural world and the lessons it teaches. There will come a time when they themselves are parents of young children and will see going outdoors as much more than blowing off steam.

MLK

Kids Can Help

Doing household chores with a parent gives the child a sense of belonging in the family circle no matter what the dynamics—a single parent, two people committed by togetherness, marriage or any combination of those living together, all of them providing care for the child. Helping and being appreciated gives the child a feeling of belonging, safety within the family circle and value. Chores can be thought of as family activities and not something one is paid for or does to earn an allowance.

Some of the simple things a young child can do to help the daily running of the home are:

Folding: towels, napkins for table setting, knits from the dryer. "Thanks, you made all of the corners straight so they'll fit in the drawer/on the shelf better."

Sorting socks, silverware from the dishwasher or draining rack, buttons, different sized nails/nuts and bolts, colors of spools of thread. "That will be a big help and save time when we're looking for something."

Food preparation: stirring ingredients, adding measured ingredients, rinsing off some fresh fruits or vegetables. "You poured so carefully—didn't spill a drop!" or, "Now we don't have to worry about the spray that may have been on the apples."

Putting away, picking up personal belongings. "You made our house look nicer by taking care of your things and not being so messy."

Doing regular chores: caring for family pets (giving water and feeding); sorting clothes for the wash; emptying the waste-baskets; separating items for the recycle bins.

If parents can spare the time and have the patience, they could allow a child as young as a preschooler to help vacuum the carpet, rake leaves, and select the wood for a DIY project.

The child may need coaching to accomplish tasks like these, but in the long run the togetherness of the experience with you will pave the way for his acceptance of the necessity of these tasks.

If you are planning a family or friends gathering during the holidays, your children will be much more content if they are in on some of the preparations. They can stir the filling for the pumpkin pies, chop the nuts with a nut-chopper, tear the bread into small pieces for the dressing, and, if you're lucky enough to have an old-fashioned meat grinder and Grandma's recipe, they can grind fresh cranberries for the cranberry relish! Of course, setting the table is something children love to do. Even though some of the silverware may have to be straightened afterward, they have it on the table, haven't they?

It's also fun for them to look forward to having guests by letting them make paper placemats and name cards. Heavy-duty shelf paper cut into lengths and designed with crayons and/or magic markers is economical, recyclable and easy to use. Cardboard index cards (3" x 5"), folded in the middle so they can stand, will work well for children to print the guests' names from a list you have for them to copy. If they are too young to print, they could put a design on the card after you have written the name.

Often they have made decorations at school or child care which they can either use or use as a model to make more at home. A good thing about entertaining family and/or close friends is that they usually do not expect elegance and can usually be counted on to appreciate the love and work that went into the children's efforts. These are the kinds of family experiences that children will tuck into their "feeling" memories. They will draw upon them again and again as adults and be thankful for their family.

GS

Sharing Cultural Events with Kids

One of the best things about being a grandparent is getting to share your enthusiasms with the next generation as well as experience these things afresh through your grandchildren's wondering eyes. But introducing very young children to cultural events that adults enjoy needs to be done carefully and thoughtfully, as one of the Grandmothers was to learn.

When she and her husband took their granddaughters to a puppet show, 8-year-old Isabelle enjoyed a delightful performance of *Peter and the Wolf,* but 3-year-old Ava anticipated only Peter and the Big Bad Animal That Scares Little Girls. Fortunately, this grandmother had told the girls the story beforehand, so Ava could make it very clear that she did not want to see any wolf—even if it was only a four-inch-high puppet. So Grandma and Ava sat on the aisle, and as soon as they heard the French horns sounding that ominous wolf's theme, out they went to the brightly lit lobby. Once the wolf had been safely dispatched by the hunters, they returned to their seats for the happy ending. Nobody called Ava a baby; no one cajoled her to stay through the scary part, saying "It's only a puppet; don't be afraid." There was simply a matter-of-fact acceptance of her wishes and reassurance that the adults respected her feelings and were willing to accommodate them.

Parents and often grandparents wish to share plays, museums and other cultural events that they enjoy with the children and may be eager to start them on a lifetime of arts appreciation as early as possible. However, this eagerness often leads to exposing children to things before they are ready and without giving the whole experience sufficient thought. For example, when taking more than one child to an event, it helps to have two adults on hand: one to exit with a child who may be scared (or need to go to the bathroom) and one to stay with those who are enthusiastically enjoying the program.

Also, it's important to choose events carefully. If it's a show in a huge theater, based on a hit movie or TV show, it's likely there will be loud noises, flashing lights, and confusing special effects, all of which can be very upsetting—even to kids as old as seven or eight. If you're going to be in one of these situations, it's best to plan an escape route. Better yet, avoid the situation altogether.

Parents know how important it is to prepare kids for new experiences, and most know to tell their child what the show will be about beforehand. But they should also consider other aspects of the experience that may be new and overwhelming, such as the cavernous arena and the large numbers of people streaming in the door.

When one of the Grandmothers took her grandchild to a Sesame Street show, her 3-year-old granddaughter did fine with the hectic business of getting to the theater and settling into her seat. Everyone was sure she was going to love the show, but when the lights went out and the hall went pitch black, she completely lost it. Screaming and crying in terror, she had to be carried out and taken home before even one beloved Muppet appeared on stage.

Trips to the museum can be lots of fun for kids, or they can be endurance tests. It's up to the adults to make sure that they're the former rather than the latter or their kids will never want to set foot in one again. It helps if you plan short excursions to exhibits that are focused on something the child is truly interested in and go back several times until the child has gotten his fill. Returning to familiar places and seeing the same exhibits is actually more educational than always seeing something new. Children need time and repetition to absorb and come to understand what they are seeing.

As with so many things in parenting, slow and steady wins the race. Parents and grandparents should try to remember that they have many years to take the kids to cultural events. Rushing it will only kill their kids' enthusiasm. You may think this is the only chance you will have to take your 4-year-old to see *The Nutcracker*, but it's not. The ballet is too long and confusing for a child so young. Better to wait until she is in second grade, when she can sit through such a long performance.

Finally, think back to what you remember about any cultural events you may have experienced as a child. We'll bet the best memories are simply of the shared pleasure of spending time together as a family. So be sure to stop for an ice cream treat after the show or have a picnic in the park after the museum visit. After all, your main objective is to help your kids become as enthusiastic about cultural events as you are. If you can leave them with a pleasant memory, they will be eager to return again and again. In time, they will begin taking their own kids and grandkids to the theater or museum, enriching the lives of generations to come.

GTR

When to Get Help

Your pediatrician says he'll outgrow it. Of course he will. He's an average kid from a good-enough family, so he will not be wearing diapers to high school, sucking on his pacifier at his college graduation ceremony, or throwing tantrums in the grocery check-out line when he goes shopping with his wife.

Of course, because he is of average good health and from a good-enough gene pool, he probably would outgrow all his childhood diseases, too, without medical intervention. But you take him for regular check-ups anyway and make sure he sees the doctor when he is sick because you don't want him to suffer the unnecessary pain and stress of an untreated illness. You don't want him to suffer the unnecessary pain and stress of an unexamined developmental conflict, either, so that's why you worry about the diapers and pacifier and tantrums, even though any number of people tell you not to worry, that he'll outgrow it.

Your mother says you worry about him too much. She means well. Some parents do tend to worry too much and need to be reminded once in a while that some problems are minor, predictable and won't last forever. Ah, but you ask, which ones?

Start with trusting your own judgment. If you are concerned, you should listen to that concern.

If you are concerned about something your child persists in doing or saying, first ask, "Is the behavior developmentally appropriate?" Even though they sound like jargon, those two words are helpful, and what they refer to are behaviors that match, very broadly, the behaviors expected of a child at your child's stage of development—not necessarily his age, because kids grow at different rates. But, for example, if your toddler bites his playmates, you can be assured that such behavior is within the normal range, although the parents of the other toddlers are not likely to smile benignly over the tooth marks on their children's arms. If your kindergartener is biting his playmates, however, this would be an issue of greater concern. By kindergarten, biting should have stopped.

The second thing you might do is try to understand, for yourself, why your child is having difficulty with—with whatever it is. Try to figure out what is going on in your child's small head and heart, why he erupts in anger or dissolves in tears or refuses to pick up his Legos. He is a child; he doesn't process information or react to setbacks or experience time the way an adult would, so often it isn't easy to figure out if he's upset over something you said twenty minutes ago or if he's worried about a larger issue—maybe that expected baby brother or sister you keep talking about with such enthusiasm. But you can observe, and listen, and make guesses, and get so in tune with him sometimes that you are feeling what he feels. And then you can talk to him about it and let him know he is understood. Just as you are consoled by a friend nodding a show of understanding over a cup of coffee, he will be comforted by your simple acknowledgment of his feelings.

But maybe you need some help in your understanding, so a third thing you might do is find a professional you can talk to—some neutral, objective person, preferably someone with whom you have (or with whom you feel you can develop) a trusting relationship. You need to talk to someone who is knowledgeable about child development, of course, but also someone who can understand your discomfort and not dismiss it; someone who will know how hard it is to hear from your child's teacher, for example, that your child is disrupting the classroom. This person should not be telling you either to ignore it (because he'll outgrow it) or, at the other extreme, that your child is clearly disturbed. Your someone needs to help you determine what the stress is that is causing your child's behavior and to work with you in order to understand what your child is feeling and why.

When you understand, what to do about it will become clear.

By listening to your child, your own concerns, and possibly the advice of a caring professional, you will no longer be waiting for your son or daughter to "outgrow it." Instead you will be better able to grow along with your child through each remarkable stage.

KSB

The Grandmothers' Wish

What quality would we Grandmothers most ardently wish for you parents of young children as the last pages of this book fade away, you ask? Well, OK, you didn't ask, but we're going to tell you anyway. Not patience, not insight, not mediation skills, not tolerance for mud and messes, not the ability to survive your busy day on three hours' sleep, not immunity to childhood illnesses, but delight. Delight in your children.

At the close of every year you've doubtless had many opportunities to observe (or at least you've heard about) Scrooge as he emerges, thrilled to be alive, after his visits from the three ghosts. Remember how he gleefully greets the boy whom he sends to get the turkey for the Cratchit family? "An intelligent boy! A remarkable boy!" he says. "What a delightful boy! It's a pleasure to talk to him." When, in fact, the boy hasn't done a thing remarkable. This is the kind of delight we would like you to be finding in your children.

Easy to dismiss that with a "Bah, humbug," or some 21st

century expression that comes more quickly to mind, we'll grant you. But hear us out.

Yes, they wear you out, both physically and mentally. Their needs are constant and usually come at inconvenient times. They whine, they fight, they demand, they throw up their grape juice onto your couch cushions. But the fact that they exist, these miniature people, and grow and change so fast and miraculously, is truly delightful. Look at how much they learn in a month, let alone a year. Wasn't he struggling to stand up only a few months ago, and now he can run! Wasn't she speaking in one-word sentences last spring, and now she talks in paragraphs! Scrooge was right—it's altogether remarkable.

If you're having trouble working up some delight in the kid who poured his chocolate milk down his best shirt right before his preschool photo will be taken, picture yourself leaning over his bed when he's asleep and the little twinge you get in the area of the heart as you contemplate how beautiful he is, how infinitely precious. Remember how teary you got when she and her classmates stood up at the child-care holiday party and sang "Rudolph the Red-nosed Reindeer"? Most of the rest of the kids were standing there scratching their bellies or singing off key, but your daughter was singing right on pitch, every word, louder than all the others. Or maybe your kid *was* one of the ones doing the scratching, but wasn't she absolutely adorable?

And think of the cute things she's said, the antics that you've described to your co-workers or called up your mom on the phone to tell her about. What about when you asked him to pick up his toys and he said, "But I just can't want to do that right now!" Remember the time that you were so sick you couldn't get out of bed, but somehow she climbed up on the kitchen counter without breaking her neck, got out the peanut butter and jelly, and made you a sandwich! Oh, and how delightful the way he looks at the world because to him it's fresh and new, and how unexpected but understandable the way he interprets what you say so literally. Ten years ago, one the Grandmothers' grandsons, when told that Aunt Irene's body was in the closed casket at her funeral, asked, after a long pause, "But where's her head?" and we're still laughing about it.

You have your own stories to tell, your own cute things your children have said, to share. Do try to look at your children through Scrooge's eyes—the transformed Scrooge, that is. Your child is without doubt the most remarkable, delightful creature on earth. Even when he's just standing there, brown stains starting to set on his shirt, his face in a guilty grin.

KSB

Who are the Grandmothers?

There are four of them. They have their ages in common, and the fact that they all have degrees in Early Childhood Education and have retired from their employment as teachers and administrators in early childhood programs. They also are mothers and grandmothers, having produced 14 children and 21 grandchildren. They have worked together for decades, but not without advice, assistance and support.

They have met together within the halls of the Hanna Perkins Center for Child Development in Cleveland, Ohio, where they have also been active attending classes, gaining insight into young children's feelings and behavior by studying with Erna Furman, world-famous child analyst and child development expert, and serving on the board of trustees of the center. When they began writing, they met primarily in the office of Barbara Streeter, the Education and Therapy Director of the Hanna Perkins School. She is a psychoanalyst, an instructor of early childhood educators and a consultant to early childhood programs in the Greater Cleveland community and throughout the country. She has always made herself available to the "Grannies" as they turned to her for help in understanding how small children learn and grow.

They are grateful to Barbara and also to Karen Goulandris, who, in her time as director of Hanna Perkins' Reinberger Parent-Child Resource Center, encouraged the Grandmothers to create pamphlets that parents could easily pick up and read on tantrums, picky eating, toilet training and more. The

Grandmothers' first fan, she helped them by providing the subject matter of most concern to young parents.

Another fan and booster was Lainie Hadden, who helped the Grandmothers reach a wider audience by introducing them to the editor of *The Plain Dealer*, which resulted in their weekly blog on the Cleveland.com website. With her formidable powers of persuasion, Lainie finally convinced them that what they had to say was worthy of becoming a book.

Kathy Smith Baker worked for twenty years as a teacher, then director, in several different child care centers, taught Early Childhood Education courses at Cuyahoga Community College, and in retirement spent two years teaching English in the Peace Corps in Romania. For several years she also taught creative writing to some of the women living in the Cuyahoga County Jail. All of the introductory material as well as more than half of the articles included here are hers.

Maria Kaiser worked for three years as a preschool teacher, seven years as a child care center director, three years as a child development director for a health care agency, and then eighteen years as a program manager and administrator for the Achievement Centers for Children. In her retirement she taught Early Childhood classes at Cuyahoga Community College and now teaches nannies and governesses. She also has been pursuing more seriously her long-term interest in photography, watercolor painting and print-making. It has been satisfying for her to hang her work in local art shows. This is her first effort as an illustrator.

Georgianna Roberts was a nursery school teacher and director, and instructor of Early Childhood Education at Cuyahoga Community College. At the Center for Human Services, she provided consultation and training for cooperative preschools, other nursery schools and child care centers. She was president of the Cleveland and Ohio chapters of the Association for the Education of Young Children and coordinated grass roots advocacy at the county and state level for Head Start and child care funding and improved licensing of early childhood programs.

Ginny Steininger taught kindergarten and spent nearly fifteen years as a teacher and director of a cooperative preschool. She subsequently became the director of the child-care program for the Cuyahoga Valley Vocational School, where she taught courses in child development and helped establish the first public preschool in Ohio for children with difficulties. She then spent sixteen years as the Education Director of Hanna Perkins School.

What is the Hanna Perkins Center for Child Development?

Hanna Perkins Center for Child Development is a non-profit organization where educators and mental-health professionals collaborate to help children understand and manage their emotions for success in school and life.

Its services include:

Hanna Perkins School: Kindergarten, Preschool, Parent/Toddler program, and EPIC Early Learning for children with Autism Spectrum Disorders.

Hadden Clinic for Children and Families: Mental health assessment, counseling and therapy from birth to 18; and treatment for new moms struggling with postpartum depression.

Consultation and training with other schools and early-learning centers.

Continuing education for early-learning educators, child caregivers, social workers, mental health professionals, and others who work with children on a daily basis.

Child psychoanalytic training: An official training program of the American Psychoanalytic Association, conducted in cooperation with the Cleveland Psychoanalytic Center.

Founded in 1951, Hanna Perkins Center is descended from one of the nation's earliest preschool programs. Founded in the late 19th century, it was operated by the Cleveland Day Nursery Association through the enthusiastic philanthropic support of the Hanna and Perkins families.

Made in the USA
Middletown, DE
11 April 2019